"This is a great, power-pac[illegible]
copyeditor and writer Blake Atwood. It's the book I'd like to have written if I wasn't so busy coaching and editing books. Wonderful, engaging, and clearly superior advice for the aspiring writer."

Mick Silva

Book Editor at MickSilva.com

"This book is fantastic. I'm an editor myself, but Blake has created an awesome resource. This is a must-have for any writer, editor or anyone who wants to communicate better."

Jim Woods

Writer at JimWoodsWrites.com

"*Why Every Author Needs an Editor* is not about some newer-better-faster-cheaper five-point system. Instead, it is filled with universal truths of the writer's (or artist's) experience, expressed in a personal and authentic way. Blake's warm and engaging voice might be just what you need to make these important principles hit home for the first time. For a new author who is struggling with that volatile mix of insecurity and hubris that artistic endeavor requires, Blake's compassionate encouragement will help you get over the finish line to make your work ready for the public."

Ellen Seltz

Author of *Mister Mottley Gets His Man*, EllenSeltz.com

DON'T FEAR THE REAPER

Why Every Author Needs an Editor

by Blake Atwood

Don't Fear the Reaper: Why Every Author Needs an Editor

Edited by Alison Frenzel

Published by AtWords Press

ISBN: 978-0-9897773-5-3

To all the authors I've read before,
and to all of their editors,
thank you.

CONTENTS

INSCRIPTION

"Death, be not proud, though some have called thee

Mighty and dreadful, for thou art not so;

For those whom thou think'st thou dost overthrow

Die not, poor Death, nor yet canst thou kill me.

From rest and sleep, which but thy pictures be,

Much pleasure; then from thee much more must flow,

And soonest our best men with thee do go,

Rest of their bones, and soul's delivery.

Thou art slave to fate, chance, kings, and desperate men,

And dost with poison, war, and sickness dwell,

And poppy or charms can make us sleep as well

And better than thy stroke; why swell'st thou then?

One short sleep past, we wake eternally

And death shall be no more; Death, thou shalt die."

— John Donne, *Holy Sonnets #10*

PREFACE

Writing is a mortal act presuming immortality. Though we will perish as writers, our words have the possibility of long outlasting us. That ought to be a humbling thought. The words you write may reverberate throughout time for a very long time.

I don't mean to scare you, but I do mean to give you pause. Taking your writing seriously means considering the fact that the words you pen may live on long after you're gone.

Do you want your words to have the greatest possibility of outliving you? Of achieving a kind of immortality?

Very few successful authors have accomplished that feat alone. In addition to support and encouragement from family, friends, and other writers, they received ample help from editors and other literary professionals. For authors seeking traditional publishing or self-publishing, an editor is an indispensable ally in your subconscious quest for immortality. Finding the right editor inevitably makes your book better, but a warning is in order, especially for first-time authors.

If you've never been edited before, you will experience a visceral reaction to the sight of your precious work slashed to pieces.

It can be a grim reaping.

In the single second you first glance at your work of art turned into an open-heart surgery gone wrong, you will not want to be open to correction. You will not want your blind spots revealed, your technical problems made known, or your gaping plot holes laid bare. The part of your soul that you poured into your book will wince. Your carefully constructed identity as a soon-to-be-published author will suffer a momentary identity crisis.

You will doubt yourself as a writer.

You will see edit after edit and wonder if your editor has turned on you.

You may see your editor as an adversary more than an ally.

You may rebel against their suggestions or give up writing altogether.

Or you may choose not to fear the reaper.

While the reaper may bring death in his wake, I believe that our physical death isn't the end of us. Rather than a foreboding bearer of bad news, the reaper is a guide who must cut us down before ferrying us to the Promised Land. Death is the final penance we serve, our last suffering before an eternal rest.

Yes, it's an outrageous metaphor for an editor's work with a writer, but there's credence to it. Being edited can be painful at times—death by a thousand edits—but such pain is worth the ultimate reward.

If you have found the right editor for your book, you will read through their changes and suggestions, and if you're humble enough to admit you have room to grow as a writer, you will begin to appreciate their edits. You will become a better writer because of their work, and your book will become a better book because of their talents.

The possibility of your words outlasting you will increase. Your words will defeat ultimate reaping. From beyond your grave, your words will shout the ultimate victory: "Death, thou shalt die."

There's no need to fear the reaper.

1

COPYEDITING ESSENTIALS

What Is a Copyeditor and Why Do I Need One?

Reaching the top of Mount Everest. Crossing the finish line of a marathon. Graduating school. Typing the last sentence of your book.

Sure, from the outside looking in, one of these occasions is not like the other. But from the inside looking out—when you breathe an immense sigh of relief as you slowly push your chair away from your desk—finishing the first draft of your book is a momentous occasion, one that should be accompanied by celebrations often reserved for mountain climbers, marathoners, and recent graduates.

When I finished the initial writing of my first book, I remember how simultaneously thrilled and exhausted I was. I'd accomplished what I'd set out to do. I wanted to publish it immediately and see the fruits of my labors grace the webpages of Amazon so the world could know I was an author.

Though I thought I'd already traveled far along the writing journey, I soon learned that a completed manuscript is only a halfway marker. I still had many steps yet to go, and the most daunting was the very next step I needed to take: finding and working with an editor.

Having known no editors at the time, this task felt like ascending Everest to take in the view for a few minutes then looking far, far below and wondering how I was ever going to find someone to help me off the mountain and back into civilization.

I needed a Sherpa to shape and guide my words.

Admittedly, I almost balked at getting an editor. Like many writers, I thought my prose was sufficiently flattering and my spellcheck quite capable of catching literary riff-raff. However, I'm still grateful that a small voice inside (and the many podcasts I'd been listening to) said that I absolutely had to invest in an editor. If nothing else, I needed to pay for copyediting and cover design.

Of the two copyeditors recommended to me, I went with the cheaper option, as I was secretly convinced my book would never turn a profit, even with the least expensive editor. However, it should also be known that I didn't just choose her because her rates were less expensive; she also had a deep knowledge about the subject of my first book. In addition to fixing my technical problems, her specialized knowledge ensured consistency within my book. After agreeing to her rates, she met my somewhat quick deadline and caught errors I never would have seen. Ultimately, her work made my book better.

As will be discussed in a later chapter, seeking out qualified editors and asking the right questions before working with them will reveal the positives (and negatives) of their knowledge and abilities. Don't always go with the cheaper editor or the most expensive editor; go with the right editor for your book.

But I may be putting the cart before the horse. If you're a first-time author, you may not even know where to find an editor or what kind of editor your book needs—and that's OK. I was once in the same position as you are now. In fact, one of my motivations for writing this book was to provide to other writers what I wish I would have had as a new author. If you'll stick with me, you'll be much better equipped to ask the right questions in order to find the best editor for your book.

For now, allow me to be your Sherpa, a guide to help you find your way.

In this chapter, I'll cover the basics of copyediting and why every author needs an editor. I'm a full-time copyeditor, so I'm utterly biased, but even before I started this career, I knew the intrinsic value of great copyediting. By the time you've read through this book, you'll feel the same way.

What is a copyeditor?

Simply put, a copyeditor edits your copy line-by-line. As such, they may sometimes be called a line editor. Copyeditors look for errors in spelling, grammar, punctuation, capitalization, word usage, and formatting. In some instances, they will also fact-check.

Essentially, copyeditors ensure that you're using "your" and "you're" correctly, that you have one space after a sentence, that your first paragraphs in a chapter aren't indented, and that you adhere to a stylebook (e.g., *The Chicago Manual of Style* for most books). They identify hundreds of issues that writers may gloss over, especially when furiously writing their first (or second, or third) draft.

Some copyeditors will take a strict "no write" approach to an author's work. They'll fix the issues cited above without rewriting or rearranging sentences. Other copyeditors may suggest better ways to phrase a sentence, or even rewrite sentences with the author's permission.

The best copyeditors seek to rid your manuscript of errors while making it more readable. They also serve to enhance the author's voice and refuse to allow their personal style to overtake a book.

Copyeditors are not developmental editors or proofreaders, although some copyeditors may offer such services as part of their editing packages. Because different editors offer a vastly different range of services, it can be confusing for authors to know what to expect from editors. It's imperative for any author to ask their editor specific questions about what type of editing they offer. Both the author and the editor need to be on the same page before any work commences so that neither party wastes the other's time or maxes out a budget. When contacting an editor, be clear about what kind of editing you're seeking.

For example, I'm a copyeditor, but I'll offer developmental suggestions if I think the book warrants them. If the book needs substantial developmental help, I'll refer the author to a developmental editor before copyediting their manuscript.

What is a developmental editor?

Developmental editors look at the big picture of the book and suggest changes in structure, tone, plot, characters, or concept. They're not concerned with the grammatical errors of your book; rather, they want to ensure the story you're telling is engaging and makes sense. They may even help you plot your story before you've started writing. Substantive editing is a close cousin to developmental editing, but substantive editors suggest changes after the book's been written. To learn much more about what developmental editors do, listen to the Rocking Self-Publishing Podcast interview with developmental editor Alida Winternheimer at blke.co/alidawin.

What is a proofreader?

Proofreaders discover the small errors and typos of a book immediately before it's published. They ensure that errors haven't infiltrated a book through multiple rounds of edits and revisions. Proofreaders are an author's last line of grammatical and formatting defense before sending their baby into the big, wide world.

Who needs a copyeditor?

Every author who wants their book to be the best it can be needs a professional copyeditor.

The editor's work cannot guarantee a bestseller, or even if the book will sell at all. No one can do that. But seeking the help of a qualified copyeditor serves multiple, beneficial purposes:

- Your eyes will be opened to your blind spots.
- You will be challenged as a writer and you will grow from that challenge.
- More often than not, your book will become leaner and more compelling.
- Your grammatical errors won't turn off readers.
- Your investment in other book-making professionals will benefit the publishing industry and elevate book creation expectations.

Why does an author need a copyeditor?

Typically, a book's editing process goes from a developmental editor to a copyeditor to a proofreader:

YOUR BEST DRAFT > DEVELOPMENTAL EDITOR > COPYEDITOR > PROOFREADER > PUBLISHED BOOK

I know what you're thinking: do I need to pay for all three?

If you can afford it, that's the best route, but if you're bootstrapping your own self-published novel, it might not be a financially sound decision. Plus, you may not want to wait for months on end for three different people to edit and proof your book.

At the very least, send your book to a copyeditor. Copyediting is necessary because it chisels away the detritus from your masterpiece. A copyeditor will see what you're blind to because you're too emotionally close and invested in the words you've toiled to put on the page. As a copywriter myself, I'm obviously biased, but good copyediting is invaluable.

If a copyeditor sees substantial content issues, they may refer you to a developmental editor. Proofreaders can often be found by asking a few of your grammatically inclined friends to read through your manuscript. Unless that's what they do for a living, they'll be honored by your request and won't charge you for their time.

In other words, not all books need developmental help, and you can likely find free proofreaders on your own. But professional copyediting is a necessity in the same vein that professional cover design is.

When authors invest money into their books, they reveal their seriousness about turning their words into an ongoing income stream, or even a writing career. Investing authors put skin in the game, effectively betting on themselves and their books to prove their worth in the marketplace. By paying others to polish their books before public release, such authors set themselves up for success instead of releasing an unedited, self-designed book that may sell well during its release week but fails to ever generate money over time. Authors who are serious about turning their writing into a career will do all they can to ensure that book sales continue every month, and part of that means having well-edited and well-designed books.

Furthermore, such an investment can be seen as a motivating challenge for the writer: "My book *will* earn this investment back." In fact, one of my early definitions of success for my first book was earning back the financial costs I had put into it. I never expected it to earn millions, but I had high hopes for the book to at least break even. That specific dollar number gave me a goal to strive for and it was thrilling to attain it, even as moderate of a goal as it was. Plus, paying professionals to help make your book better introduces you to some of the nicest and talented wordsmiths and graphic designers who truly enjoy what they do.

When does an author need a copyeditor?

An author needs a copyeditor when he or she has finished writing the entirety of their book, but an author *should not wait until then to contact an editor.*

Editors typically work on multiple projects, and they may not have time to fit your 120,000-word epic fantasy novel into their schedule if you wait until you've finished writing to contact them. The earlier you can contact your editor of choice and provide the details of your manuscript to them, the better likelihood you'll have of earning a place on their schedule that also fits your schedule.

What information should an author send to a copyeditor?

When reaching out to a copyeditor, you will earn his or her deep appreciation by sending these details when inquiring about their services and schedule:

Contact information: Include your email, phone, or Skype details. Some editors prefer digital face-to-face conversations before commencing work. Skyping or other forms of video conversation also allows you to ask pointed questions about what you can expect to receive from the editor.

Total word count: If necessary, send an estimated range, like 50,000 to 60,000 words. Editors charge per word, per page, or per hour, and knowing the total word count is an essential part of their estimate.

Deadline: Include the date by which you would like to receive all completed edits. If you've written a book-length manuscript of 50,000 words or more, *don't* ask for a week's turnaround time. Some editors will charge a rush fee depending on how quickly you want your book edited.

Fiction or nonfiction: Some editors only work on one or the other.

Genre: Some editors specialize in certain genres.

Type of editing: Be specific with the type of editing you think your book needs, whether developmental editing, copyediting, or proofreading. Don't hesitate to ask for what you specifically need, even if the editor you're contacting doesn't list a particular ability on their website or business card. They may offer further services (like ghostwriting or light developmental help) for reduced rates as part of a combination package of services. If not, they may be able to refer you to a qualified editing professional, saving you time in that you don't have to search for and qualify a different type of editor. As you'll read over and over again in this short book, *communicate your needs and desires up front so that both parties know what's needed and expected.*

Where can an author find a qualified copyeditor?

You're more compelled to read a book by an unknown author when a friend or trusted source recommends the book. The same holds true with finding capable copyeditors. Ask your writing friends who they've used, or email an author in your genre for a suggestion.

The only problem with this approach is that you may discover a popular copyeditor who's too busy with work to take on any new clients. If that happens, ask that copyeditor to refer you to a copyeditor they know and trust. Like writers, editors network with one another and often give referrals. Editing organizations like editcetera also exist throughout the country, and a well-defined, localized search on Google will help you find such groups.

As for online searches, check LinkedIn for copyeditors with whom you may have a 1st-, 2nd-, or 3rd-degree connection. That's an easy way to discover a personal recommendation as you can ask your mutual connection about that editor's abilities. Peruse Writer.ly's talent search, or search for editing groups on Facebook or Google+ and ask for recommendations. Literary agents sometimes publish their recommended editors as well, like Rachelle Gardner does at RachelleGardner.com/freelance-editors.

Lastly, I'd be remiss to not mention my own site, BlakeAtwood.com.

How does a copyeditor work with an author?

Most editors will request your manuscript as a Word document. Once received, they'll make changes using "Track Changes" in Word. That feature affords you the ability to click a checkmark or an X on every single item the editor changes, meaning that the author has the final say as to what edits are acceptable.

"Track Changes" also allows the editor to insert comments throughout the text. Every edit, deletion, addition, and comment appears on the right-hand side of the page. "Track Changes" also lets the viewer (whether author or editor) see the final manuscript with or without markup, Word's term for edits. This allows the author to see every single change an editor has made to his or her manuscript.

Outside of the technicalities of editing, every editor has their own way of working with an author.

If possible, some prefer to meet in person before starting work. Some like to chat via Skype, while others are content with gathering details about the project through email.

Some editors may send chapters back to the author as they finish editing each chapter, while other editors may wait until the entire manuscript has been edited before sending it back.

Some editors may offer a few hours of Q&A where an author can ask, "Why did you suggest that change here?" Yet other editors merely communicate to the author using their comments on the manuscript.

Some editors may want full payment up front, while others may ask for half up front and half on completion. Still others may offer you a payment plan based on the length of the project. Some editors may want a check in the mail, while others may be fine with payment through PayPal.

What all of this means to you as an author is that you shouldn't be afraid to ask very specific questions about the way your editor works and how they want to be paid.

If you're ever unclear about what to expect, it's better to ask than to assume.

How much does copyediting cost?

Copyediting costs vary widely. According to the Editorial Freelancers Association rates page (www.the-efa.org/res/rates.php), basic copyediting at 5–10 pages per hour ranges from $30–40 per hour. The publishing industry standard for words on a page is 250, so seeking copyediting for a 50,000-word book from a fast, though inexpensive, copyeditor ($30 per hour at ten pages per hour for twenty hours of work) would be $600. If you sought copyediting from a slow, though more costly, copyeditor, the total cost would be $1600 ($40 per hour at five pages per hour for forty hours of work).

At $1000, that's a significant difference in price, although the end product edited by both of these types of professionals may not be so different in quality. It is imperative for you to research and seek qualified recommendations for a professional editor. As for self-publishers, you want to see the best return on your investment, and that means finding a top-notch editor at a price that won't deplete your bank account.

The EFA rates page reports heavy copyediting fees ranging from $40-50 an hour at only 2-5 pages edited per hour and developmental editing at $45-55 an hour at 1-5 pages edited per hour. However, these numbers only provide rough estimates. The only way to truly know what your editing cost will be is to ask for a quote from a professional copyeditor. If you provide them with the information I previously mentioned, they should be able to quickly give you a cost and deadline estimate.

Find your Sherpa.

Relish the achievement of completing your manuscript, but realize that descending the mountain and sharing your polished words with the world is an essential series of steps required of every professional author. Though I'd be grateful to consider copyediting your book, I wholeheartedly encourage you to find a professional copyeditor that can help guide your book and shape it into an error-free masterpiece ready for publishing. Your book will be better because of it and you will definitely grow as a writer through the process.

Now that you understand the basics of copyediting, there are particular problems you can fix yourself. You can and should fix your consistent writing problems, but you can't fix the problems you can't see. The following chapter may be eye-opening for you, but even in learning how to self-edit better, allow me to sound the constant refrain of this book: *every author* (and even those who self-edit well) *needs an editor*.

2

YOUR FIRST LINE OF DEFENSE

10 Steps to Better Self-Editing

In the few months following my transition to full-time freelance work as an editor, I witnessed at least a dozen simple mistakes that all writers (including myself) can fix on their own. While self-editing is often creativity-destroying when writing your first draft, wise writers would do well to work through the following suggestions before sending their manuscript to a professional editor or to their beta readers.

In addition to making you more aware of your grammatical blind spots, self-editing may even save you money if your editor works on a per-hour basis. And even though editors love to display their knowledge, they also like reading grammatically correct manuscripts. When you show that you're a capable and confident writer who makes few mistakes, you may just endear yourself to an editor, which will allow you to delete "Find an editor" from your publishing to-do list for your next book. Furthermore, your beta readers or Advanced Reader Copy (ARC) reviewers will be grateful for the care you took in creating a readable early draft.

Now, let's get practical.

1. Rest your manuscript.

When you've finished typing the last word of your masterpiece, set it aside for a few days. If you can stand it, set it aside for a week or more. Essentially, you want to try to forget everything you've written, so that when you do come back to self-edit, the book almost seems as if someone else wrote it. You want new eyes, and the best way to do that is to rid your mind of what it's been consumed by for so long.

2. Print your manuscript, or read it out loud.

In *On Writing Well*, William Zinsser wrote, "Examine every word you put on paper. You'll find a surprising number that don't serve any purpose." For some, seeing their digitized words on paper helps them discover useless words and catch errors they otherwise wouldn't have seen.

We can also go beyond paper in order to ferret out our useless words and errant grammar and usage. For many writers, hearing the text spoken aloud makes mistakes unmistakable.

You can enlist a (very patient) friend to read it to you, or you can go the friendship-saving route and use a number of apps to have your book read to you in a semi-robotic voice.

In writing podcasts I've listened to, Voice Dream Reader has been touted as a great option for iOS users. An iOS user can also turn on VoiceOver (www.apple.com/accessibility/ios/voiceover/), though this affects all actions on the device. Amazon offers a feature for Kindle devices called Read Aloud with Voice Over (blke.co/11sXabv). Lastly, searching for "text to speech" or "read to me" on any of the app stores should lead you in the right direction.

3. Search for troubling words.

All writers have specific words and phrases that (which?) always cause them to (too?) second-guess whether (weather?) they're (their?) using them correctly. If you know what your (you're?) troubling words are, use your word processor's search function to locate every possible variant of that word or phrase.

To help you consider what your troubling words might be, here's a good starting list, excerpted from the first chapter of *Grammar Girl's Quick and Dirty Tips for Better Writing* (http://blke.co/1zUQyhW):

- a lot / alot
- affect / effect
- can / may
- further / farther
- good / well
- i.e. / e.g.
- into / in to
- it's / its
- lay / lie
- less / fewer
- that / who
- their / they're / there
- then / than
- who / whom
- your / you're

If you're unsure of how to properly use these words, there's no shame in looking it up. Grammar Girl likely has the answer.

4. Remove or replace your crutch words.

Do you know the top ten words you use most frequently in your manuscript? Outside of necessary articles and prepositions, you may be surprised at what words you tend to use over and over.

Scrivener, my preferred writing software, makes it simple to discover your crutch words. In Scrivener's top menu, go to "Project > Text Statistics," then click on the arrow next to "Word frequency." If necessary, click the "Frequency" header twice to sort your words by frequency. You'll then be presented with what could be a jarring list of the words you might be overusing. (To include your entire manuscript in the frequency count, be sure to have your entire manuscript selected in Scrivener's Binder.)

For Microsoft Word users, a free Word Usage and Frequency add-in (blke.co/1vwO46b) has been created, but other, less technical online solutions may also help, like TextFixer.com's Online Word Counter (blke.co/1tlot52) or WriteWords' Word Frequency Counter (blke.co/1wO46wX).

No matter how you determine your crutch words, go back through your manuscript and see where you can remove or replace them.

5. Remove all double spaces at the end of sentences.

If tapping two spaces following your sentence is an age-old habit ingrained into you since before the dawn of modern digital typography, may I suggest ingraining another practice? Conduct a find-and-replace after you're done writing. In Word, type two spaces in "find" and one space in "replace" and hit enter. Voila! You just time-traveled your manuscript into the 21st-century.

6. Search for problematic punctuation.

Are you a comma chameleon, adapting that otherwise innocent punctuation mark to do work it was never meant to do? Or does your manuscript need a "semicolonoscopy," a thorough checkup on proper semicolon and colon placement? If you know you have trouble with certain punctuation marks, conduct a search for that mark and learn if you're using it correctly or not. If you're still unsure, let your editor fix any misusages, but make a note to ask why they fixed the problematic punctuation. Take advantage of your investment in your editor and learn what you can while you can.

7. Run spell check.

I think writers become too accustomed to the colorful squiggles on their digital pages. I know I do. In an effort to get ideas on the page, we might run rampant over grammar and usage. Yet, those squiggles mean something. At the very, very, very least, run spell check before sending your manuscript to an editor or beta reader. It's a built-in editor that I'm not sure every writer uses to their advantage.

8. Subscribe to *The Chicago Manual of Style*

When an editor returns your manuscript back to you, they may cite particular sections of *The Chicago Manual of Style*. If you're unfamiliar with this Bible of the publishing industry, you may not be aware of precisely why the editor made a certain change. By subscribing to CMOS (it's only $35 a year), you'll be able to look up issues on your own *before* sending your manuscript off to an editor or beta reader.

Sure, you shouldn't get too hung up on some of the issues (editors have their jobs for a reason), but learning more about the mechanics of writing can only help you become a better writer. You can also buy the hardback version of *The Chicago Manual of Style*, but I recommend the online version for its ease of use.

9. Format accordingly.

While preferred styles may differ from one editor to the next, you can show your professionalism by formatting your manuscript to industry standards. Such formatting makes it easier for beta readers to consume, and editors prefer industry-standard formatting, which allows them more time to edit your actual words instead of tweaking your formatting. Here are some basic formatting tips:

- Send your manuscript as a Word document (.doc / .docx).
- Use a single space following periods.
- Use black, 12-point, Times New Roman as the font.
- Use double-spaced line spacing. If you've already written your book with different line spacing, select all of your text in Word, click Format > Paragraph, then select "Double" in the drop down box under "Line spacing."
- Don't hit tab to indent paragraphs. In Word, select all of your text, then set indentation using Format > Paragraph. Under "Indentation" and by "Left," type .5. Under "Special," choose "First line" from the dropdown menu.

- The first paragraph of any chapter, after a subheader, or following a bulleted or numbered list *shouldn't* be indented.
- Use page breaks between chapters. In Word, place the cursor at the end of a chapter, then click "Insert > Break > Page Break" in Word's top menu. Don't just keep hitting return until you create a new page.

10. Don't over-edit.

Set aside an hour or two to go through this list, but be careful about over-editing. You may start seeing unnecessary trees within your forest of words, but you don't want to raze to the ground what you've toiled so hard to grow. There's a middle path between exhausting yourself in a vain attempt for perfection and being too lazy to run spell check. Do yourself and your book a favor and self-edit, but be careful to not go overboard.

If you're creating a professional product, your self-edits shouldn't be your last line of defense against grammatical errors. In other words, I don't offer this chapter to write myself out of a job. Even while going through the self-editing steps above, you'll still need an editor to ensure that your manuscript is as polished as possible. You will still miss errors. Plus, going through the editing process with a professional editor will help you become a better self-editor the next time you write a book.

3

HOW TO MAKE AN EDITOR LOVE YOU

10 Guidelines to Best Prep Your Book for Editing

A healthy writer/editor relationship will be reflected in the final version of your book. A vast majority of your readers won't know this, but a trusting author/editor relationship *always* leads to a better book. More than just catching the spelling and grammar mistakes that spell check missed, a capable and qualified editor chisels away what *isn't* your book.

For an editor to know what shouldn't be in the final version of your book, they need to know and trust you as the author. An editor should know your hopes for the book, your target audience, the message you're attempting to get across, as well as any stylistic choices you have made that cut against the grain of standard grammar, usage, or formatting. Essentially, the more information you can provide to them about your book, the better they will understand how to pare down the book so that its focus is razor-sharp.

So, how can you gain such trust quickly to get the best return on your investment in an editor?

While there is always a certain luck of the draw when an author begins working with a new editor, putting specific practices into place will make any editor love a writer. If you can present the best version of your book to an editor, they'll be much more inclined to take on your project. Remember, editors are readers too, and they enjoy well-written books, even if they're ones they have to edit. When you send a polished (not perfect) manuscript to an editor that contains an engaging story—and the nonfiction genre needs compelling stories too—you'll make your editor's work much more enjoyable.

Let's consider these ten practices you can incorporate into your process so that when you finally do send your beloved manuscript off to an editor, they'll be thrilled to help make your book shine. In the list that follows, I'm assuming you have a good grasp of the English language and that you've written a complete manuscript.

1. Take a break.

You've read this before, but it bears repeating. Now that you've put in months and possibly even years into writing your book, stash your manuscript in a drawer. It doesn't matter if that drawer is real or digital. Just remove your book from your presence for a week. If you can bear it, hide it from yourself for at least two weeks. If you have the patience of a Zen master, forget about it for a month. Try as hard as you can to let what you've worked on so assiduously erase itself from the deepest recesses of your mind.

If you find yourself waking up in the middle of the night thinking about a better way to frame the conflict in Chapter 16, you haven't rested your manuscript long enough. Go back to sleep and tell your mind that you've finished your book … for now. (Yes, you'll probably want to make a note of that change for future reference, but *only* if the change is *certainly* for the better.) If you've waited a week but still find yourself constantly thinking about how you can better your book, try to give yourself another week without touching your manuscript in any way.

The goal is to erase the memory of your book. I know that might be challenging considering the time you've invested, but I believe this is an essential strategy to having a better book and presenting a more polished work to an editor. When you allow yourself to forget what you have written, you create emotional distance from your text. This resting period, whether it's a week or a month, allows you to eventually return to your manuscript with fresh eyes, as if you were the book's first reader and as someone who doesn't intimately know the book's content. Of course, this can never be wholly true as you will always be heavily emotionally invested in your words, but a resting period can at least approximate the new reader experience.

2. Read your book.

Once your self-imposed manuscript banishment period has ended, attempt to read your book as an objective reader. Try to forget that you're the book's author. Read it with an eye toward the broad issues of every book. Consider its audience, purpose, and scope. Who is the book speaking to? What is the book ultimately saying? Could more (or less) be said?

Like writing a first draft, your first read through ought to be more focused on flow rather than fixing. In other words, don't get bogged down in grammar, spelling, and formatting issues. After all, you'll be paying someone to help fix those. But, if you do see consistent errors in any of those areas, you'd do well to make a note of that and fix them later.

However, you should try to act more like a developmental editor on your first read through by exploring answers to the following questions.

If nonfiction:

- Does your book flow?
- Do your arguments make sense?
- Are your examples compelling?
- Are there parts that seem to float in space, untied to anything else in the book?
- What could be expanded upon?
- Do segues need to be written?

If fiction:

- Could your characters be more strongly defined?
- Are you showing more than telling?
- Does the pace of the book feel natural to the story you're telling?
- Does enough conflict exist throughout the book to make situations interesting?
- Is your underlying message conveyed?

For absolutely any kind of book:

- What parts bore you?
- What parts confuse you?
- What parts engage you?

When you have a strong emotional response to something you've written, your reader may as well. So, when you find yourself thinking about something else entirely while reading *your own words*, it's probable that a reader will also be turned off by that section.

Fortunately, this works for the converse as well: when you find yourself wholly absorbed by a certain passage, your readers will likely find themselves engaged as well. Thus, this reaction could be a sign for you to expand upon that particular section, or more fully define that character, or increase the tension.

As you read, make quick notes for developmental issues you spot. The end goal with this step is to be able to send an engrossing book to an editor, one that may not be free of all grammatical errors, but whose base content tells a compelling story. If you accomplish this step well, it's less likely that a copyeditor will refer you to a developmental editor.

Attempting to be your own developmental editor is very difficult, especially if you're a new author. That's why developmental editors exist. Because they see a broad range of works-in-progress, they have a better understanding of what's missing in terms of characterization, setting, or plot. Additionally, they are more objective about your book because they don't share your emotional closeness to it.

If you have trouble assessing whether your book is engaging or tells a complete story, by all means hire a developmental editor. The suggestions provided at the beginning of this section are simply to help you think through some of the broader issues of your book after you've finished writing it. If you find it challenging to answer those questions, you may need to hire developmental help. (Note: nonfiction books can also benefit from investing in a developmental editor. Just be sure that they have prior experience in nonfiction developmental editing.)

Once you've given proper consideration to the flow of your book, conduct another read-through with regard to the ten self-editing steps provided in the previous chapter. If you find yourself committing a multitude of grammatical sins, or if you don't know what to look for when it comes to common grammar errors, buy *Grammar Girl's Quick & Dirty Tips for Better Writing*. If you can ensure that your book *doesn't* contain the errors she lists, you're making your copyeditor's job easier, as well as becoming a better writer yourself.

3. Learn proper formatting.

The manuscript you send to an editor doesn't have to be publish-ready, but it should be properly formatted per industry standards. Unless you're working in a specialized format like a screenplay, what you send to an editor should be formatted as listed in Step 9 of the previous chapter.

Two caveats: You won't lose most editors if your manuscript isn't strictly formatted as I've suggested, but you will endear yourself to them if you present a professional-looking book. This formatting makes reading easier on the eye, and it may even save you money since the editor won't have to spend their time adjusting your formatting so they can get to the business of proper editing.

I mentioned Word's functions because Word is still a de facto word processor for a majority of writers. Personally, I use and highly recommend Scrivener (blke.co/11UTPBZ). Regardless of what program you use to compose your masterpiece, learn how to properly format and export your manuscript in alignment with the basic formatting tips I've presented. Though it may take you a few hours to learn proper formatting in your word processor, the future benefits far outweigh the present cost in time. Remember that writing is a constant growth process, and that includes growing in your ability to use writing technology as best as you can.

4. Do your homework.

You've already written an entire book, which equates to having written multiple term papers for months on end. So why am I advocating *more* homework? Because conducting basic research on who you want to edit your book will help you spend less time trying to get someone to edit your book.

You want to find the right kind of editor, and "right" means many things. First, you ought to know what kind of editing your book may need. Copyeditors don't want to waste their time on books that need developmental help, but developmental editors are fine with reading through books that need copyediting help. Remember, the editing process typically goes from a developmental editor to a copyeditor to a proofreader.

If you think your plot or overall structure might need help, find a developmental editor. If you just need help with grammar, spelling, and similar problems you may not have caught, find a copyeditor. If you're absolutely convinced that your story is engaging and your grammar is impeccable, hire a proofreader. At the very least, you should hire one of these types of professionals. They will help polish your book so it's ready for publication.

To find a qualified editor, I suggest talking to other writers in your genre to hear who they've used and recommend. Word-of-mouth marketing is fast and effective, and you're much more likely to trust a fellow writer's recommendation. Writers' groups, both those that meet online and in the real world, are fantastic for a number of reasons, including the fact that they can help you locate an editor. Such groups may even have editors as members. Still, you need to do your homework to ensure that the editor is the kind of editor you need.

If you don't belong to a writer's group, search LinkedIn for "editor" or "copyeditor." You'll specifically want to look for editing professionals who are connected to someone you already know. That way, you can ask your connection whether they might recommend that editor. If you don't have a first- or second-degree connection to an editor, localize your LinkedIn search and consider meeting a possible editor face-to-face. More often than not, if they want your business, they won't charge for an initial meeting.

Once you've found the right kind of editor for your project, be sure you know how they want to receive your manuscript. Most will request a Word document. Some may even offer a free edit of a small number of pages, both so they can get a feel for your work and vice-versa. You may even consider being proactive and requesting a free edit, but don't ask for an edit of more than 1250 words. When an editor offers this, jump on the opportunity. More often than not, you're *not* agreeing to work with them by accepting their offer of a free edit. Since the free edit is used as a barometer of both party's skills, either party can back out of the arrangement before any contract has been signed.

Doing your homework on possible editors is a smart, cost-effective move. While it may take time to research the type, quality, cost, and other details in locating a quality editor, the investment should pay off in droves, especially once you've found an editor who clicks with you and is anxious to work with you on future projects. If you put in the time to find a professional editor for your first book, you're likely saving yourself a significant amount of time for when you're ready to have your second book edited.

5. Be timely.

A client who fails to appreciate an editor's schedule will likely not be that editor's client for long. Editors often work on multiple projects at the same time, whether that's editing other books, writing their own books, or freelancing in other ways. Consequently, they may have more deadlines than you as an author might have. And while it would be nice to believe that your book is always their top priority, that's simply not the case. Busy editors (who tend to be the *good* editors) juggle projects, shifting their prioritized work day-by-day. Some days, your book will be their top priority. Other days, someone's book with a closer deadline will replace it. Regardless, an editor can't do their job unless the author holds up their end of the contract as well.

This means that the author should respond to an editor's comments or questions within a reasonable timeframe. In Kelly James-Enger's book on ghostwriting, *Goodbye Byline: Hello Big Bucks*, (blke.co/1yTfrtJ), she relates that she gives her clients five business days to respond to her requests. To me, that's generous, because five days waiting is often five days of *not* working on that client's book. But she also takes into account that many of her ghostwriting clients are busy professionals who have hired her because they don't have the time to write a book. Consequently, she knows they may not be able to answer her within a day or two.

However, I think most aspiring writers—and especially those keen to publish their first book—would want to respond to an editor within one or two days. Such timely responses allow the editor to dive back into your book.

Editors also appreciate timeliness in payment. Once you've received a contract from an editor, read it thoroughly to know how much you're paying, when you need to make those payments, and how the editor accepts payment. If anything is unclear, contact the editor directly. Again, you want to ensure that both sides fully understand the working relationship *before* any work commences.

Payment schedules vary, as some editors may request full payment up front while others may ask for half up front and half upon completion. Still other editors may ask for a third up front, a third following the first round of edits, and the last third after a final draft has been submitted back to the author. For longer projects, an editor might request payment per each chapter edited. That's why it's vitally important to your bank account and the health of your editor/author relationship that you carefully read your contract in regard to payment.

Editors work to excel at keeping to a schedule and meeting deadlines. They like seeing that in their clients as well.

6. Be available.

This instruction is closely related to what you just read. Being timely means responding to your editor's requests within a timeframe agreed upon by the both of you. Consequently, timeliness means being available. If you're a busy professional trying to eke out a book in the margins of your life, this can be a daunting task, but understand that your editor can't finish your book until they've received feedback from you.

Before even beginning the editing process, communicate with your editor about how and when you'd like to be contacted. Most interactions can occur via email with the edited document sent back and forth, but some issues are better solved through talking. When an editor isn't quite sure what you meant by a particular word or phrase, they may want to discuss that with you, especially if it's a key phrase in the book. When an editor might have a suggestion to make your book better, they may want to discuss that with you in order to hear your take on their idea. There are dozens of reasons why an editor might want to contact you, and you will get the most out of your investment by making yourself available to them.

For instance, an editor may want to clarify particular style choices, like when a character speaks with a certain dialect represented by nonstandard spelling and punctuation. An editor may need to know unwritten backstory to ensure that a character is holding true to who they are. An editor may want to know why you use a particular word over and over again. Was it on purpose for a certain effect, or is it just a bad habit? These are only a few examples, but any number of issues can make themselves known as an editor works through your manuscript. By answering their questions quickly (within two days at least), you can ensure that you're getting the most out of your investment.

Of course, editors understand that you have a schedule and other responsibilities as well. They'll work with you to find a suitable time and avenue to communicate with you. Many freelance editors will even go so far as to talk with you after traditional business hours, especially if you have a full-time job. Like any good working relationship, it's a give-and-take that requires flexibility on the part of both the author and the editor. Plus, you'll endear yourself to your editor if you regularly make yourself available and seldom miss an appointment.

7. Be honest.

Here's the truth: an editor is going to be brutally honest about your work. They may make so many changes to your manuscript that you might ask yourself whether it's even the same book (something we'll cover in a later chapter).

But always remember that it's *your* book. Unless they're fixing a black-and-white grammatical issue, editors aren't telling you what to do; rather, they're making knowledgeable and well-intentioned suggestions they believe will make your book better. In other words, they're being honest about their assessment of your work.

This ought to go both ways.

Trust is built on honesty, so don't hold back on your own feedback. When a suggested change doesn't jibe with your voice or plot, speak up.

Editors like to see authors defend their work with reasonable arguments. When this kind of interaction happens, it often leads to a better book, and both the author and editor learn more about each other. It can sometimes be a difficult process, especially if one party is adamant about their opinion, but you will fail to serve your book well if you're not its first and foremost champion.

Remember: no one else will fight for your book's vision. If an editor suggests a change you don't agree with, say so. By biting your tongue because you're working with a professional, you may harbor silent bitterness toward them. Don't allow time for such a seed to grow.

At the first instance of sensing a disagreement with one of your editor's choices, kindly let them know about it and then be prepared for an honest discussion about the merits of your argument.

Your editor will expect you to be able to take criticism; you should expect the same of them when necessary.

8. Be patient.

Proper editing takes time. According to the Editorial Freelancers Association rates, some editors charge an hourly fee based on the number of 250-word pages they can edit per hour. Depending on the type of editing, an editor can work through one to ten pages per hour. If you send your 80,000-word book (320 pages) to a copyeditor capable of working on ten pages per hour, it will take that editor thirty-two hours to complete your edit.

"That's less than a typical week's worth of work," you may think. That's both true yet not. Remember, editors typically work on projects for multiple clients (and themselves). If they allot two hours per day to the project mentioned above, it will take them sixteen business days to finish editing your book. That's half a month, and that doesn't include lulls in the work while they seek feedback from you (see Points 6 and 7 above).

When considering your book's launch date, be sure to include enough time in your publishing schedule for your editor of choice to complete their work. Be clear on your deadline expectations so that you can receive your manuscript back in time in order to meet your launch date. Unfortunately, you may run into unexpected setbacks—your editor may get sick for a week, for instance—

so you might also want to consider adding an extra week of padding to your publishing timeline.

As an author, co-author, and ghostwriter, I understand the deep urge that some writers have to publish quickly. As soon as a "good enough" draft is finished, writers want to release it so they can start blasting their social networks with proof that they're an author. That's not necessarily a bad thing, but it's also not the best thing.

What's better than a one-day push toward literary approval is building a career out of your words by taking the time to create polished work. This means working as hard as you can on your own, then seeking help from editing and book design professionals. With more than 3,500 new books appearing on Amazon *every day*, you can't afford to rush your book to market. It will get its lunch eaten and be forgotten by dinner.

As hard as it is, be patient with the process.

9. Be open.

In an interview with *The New York Times*, author E.L. Doctorow said, "Writing is an exploration. You start from nothing and learn as you go." In the interview compilation book *Writers at Work*, he also likened writing to "driving a car at night. You never see further than your headlights, but you can make the whole trip that way."Taken together, those two quotes aptly summarize the ever-leaning-into-learning life of a writer.

I'd have to imagine that even an author as renowned as Doctorow would agree that he hasn't "made it" as a writer. Sure, he's made it insofar as creating a life and career out of his words, but if we're talking about mastering the craft of writing as "making it," I'd have to believe that few, if any, successful writers ever think they've achieved "maximum writerliness."

There's always more to learn.

This news should encourage you. Every author wrestles with words, and as soon as they've finished one book, many would claim that starting the next book feels like beginning from ground zero all over again. Still, because they've completed writing one book, they've learned an immense amount about the project itself, *as well as about themselves.* It's because of this continuous growth of self and craft that the writer must always be learning. They don't stay the same and neither does the world around them. The jots and tittles of writing may always remain constant, but the infinite variations a writer can concoct from letters, words, and ideas require an ongoing openness to the craft.

This lofty idea crashes back to reality when you receive your bleeding manuscript back from an editor. In that singular moment, you may want to hold your barely breathing manuscript close to your chest, whisper "My precious," then never contact your editor again. That's OK, but it's not OK to stay in that position. In a later chapter, we'll discuss much more about that first reaction to being edited, but for now, know that being open to becoming a better writer—and being open to even the most heinous of edits—is a character trait of all serious writers.

10. Offer affirmation.

Lastly, a simple thank you goes a long way. When you've received your final edits, say thanks.

With social media, this ought to be an easy task that requires little of you but could mean much to an editor. Whether you're self-publishing or are being traditionally published, there are hundreds of book publishing professionals that work behind the scenes to ensure that the books you read are error-free, well-designed, and enticingly priced. They know that their accolades from authors and readers might be few and far between, but when they come, they're much appreciated.

Plus, when you encourage your editor, you enhance their professional view of you, which could result in faster turnaround, priority scheduling, or even a discount.

There's one thing editors like more than simple

affirmation though: referrals. If you've experienced a helpful editing process and you believe your book is better for having been edited, shout it from the rooftops. Tell your writer friends and connections about your editor. Post status updates leading to his or her website. Be specific in your praise. Consider sending your editor an endorsement quote that he or she could use in their marketing materials. (Plus, when you do this, you're also getting your name and book listed on another website, and that's always helpful.)

Though it doesn't always happen, editors who receive such encouraging words may be more prone to returning the favor by posting their own social media updates when your book comes out or recommending your book to their connections. Realize too that experienced editors may have connections with agents, acquisition editors, or other literary professionals. In other words, a good relationship with a connected editor could result in your book being seen by that one person who could change your life.

I can't guarantee that your author/editor relationship will be without its challenges, but if you follow these ten guidelines, I can guarantee that you will endear any prospective editor to you and your book.

Now that we know a few of the major issues that can help you land a great editor, what *shouldn't* you do?

4

HOW TO MAKE AN EDITOR NOT LIKE YOU SO MUCH

7 Ways to Incite an Editor

Regardless of the horror stories you may have heard from your writer friends, editors are people too. Consequently, they will react to you and your book as humans do: in a fascinatingly wide array of ways. As you read in the previous chapters, there are a few simple steps you can take to ensure that your book has its best chance of being worked on by a capable editor.

But the opposite exists as well. There are a few simple ways you can prevent your book from ever being seen by a qualified editor, or from establishing a healthy writer/editor relationship that could lead to better books over the lifetime of your writing career.

1. Send an uncooked book.

If you're not at least 90 percent certain that the book you're sending to an editor is the best first- or second-draft version you can send to them, *don't send it.*

As far as I'm aware, most writers struggle with shipping. Of the more perfectionistic, they'll want to get their manuscript as close to perfect as possible before allowing anyone else to read one word of it. Yet other writers exist on the opposite end of that spectrum, ones who consider a rough draft with a good-enough story to be fine for publication. The key is to find the happy medium, the place where the author knows that some work still needs to be accomplished, but is confident enough in their own craft and storytelling ability that they can release it to an editor.

When a writer sends a pre-baked book to an editor, they're wasting their own time as well as the editor's. When the editor receives the book and sees that grammar mistakes abound in every other sentence, or that the story fails to make sense, or that the author didn't even think to run spell check, the editor will send the manuscript back to the author. That's at least a week, if not sometimes a month, that both the author and the editor could have put to better use.

"But how will I know when my book is ready to be sent to an editor?"

This question is especially pertinent for writers just beginning to get serious about publishing their words for a wider audience. In many ways, sending your book to an editor is like trying out for *American Idol*. You don't want to be that kid who earnestly believes he can sing but is then dramatically—and very publicly—proven otherwise. Unfortunately, there are far too many creatives who ardently believe in their talent and yet have never received honest feedback about their supposed gift. What makes this process even more difficult is the absolutely subjective nature of it. One person may hate an author's style while it may resonate with millions of other readers.

But back to the question at hand: how do you know when a book is good enough to send to a copyeditor? This is where kind, though honest, friends and family members can help. Before spending money on a professional edit, ask a dozen or so of your close connections to read through your book. Ask them basic questions like:

- Did the story or topic interest you?
- Did you learn something?
- Did you see any repeated grammar errors?
- Did the book make sense?
- Would you buy this book?

By keeping your questions simple and few, you'll be sure to receive answers that can help you deduce whether or not it's time to take the next step in the publishing process. At all times, ask for *honest* feedback. Be sure to reiterate that your readers won't hurt your feelings based on their responses to your questions.

Yes, some of these responses *will* actually hurt, but we'll talk about what to do with that in a later chapter. What you're trying to get as far away as possible from is having any of your readers' opinions biased by the fact that they know you. That can be a challenge, but it's one of the few and *free* ways to get someone else's general take on your book.

If you're not comfortable with having friends and family see an early version of your book, join a writer's group online or in real-life and request a few people to read through your book, asking them the same questions as above. Just be warned though: writer's groups can result in highly critical opinions that can sometimes do more damage than good. Because they don't know you as well as your friends and family, there's much less holding them back from releasing their full and sometimes blunt opinions.

If you're brave, maybe the best route to assessing the quality of an early draft is to ask some friends and family, as well as people in your writer's group, to review the book. Since you can assume (I hope) that your family and friends are biased toward positively reviewing your book and that your writer's group may be more critical in their reviews, looking at the median of their collective responses should yield a realistic glimpse into where your book may be falling short. In other words, if both groups agree that a particular chapter was boring, or that a character was unbelievable (and not in a good way), or that the ending didn't make sense, you know you have a problem that needs help.

As I said before, if you're not 90 percent sure that your book could be better in some broad capacity, don't send it to an editor. Find someone you know that could offer you an honest and free read through to help you assess whether your next step should be to hire an editor.

2. Request constant attention.

If you've located an editor and have signed a contract with them, don't be pushy. Know what deadlines the two of you have agreed upon and abide by those deadlines. You don't want to be the author who constantly nags an editor regarding when your book will be finished. The editor will waste time replying to your emails rather than working on your book!

This is where trust comes into play, which is one of the most important aspects of an author/editor relationship. Trusting your editor to capably finish your edits on time requires trust, and this can be a difficult process for first-time authors working with their first editor, especially if the author has already set a book launch date. (If you do set a book launch date before seeking an editor, make absolutely sure that your editor knows your launch date!)

Don't be the person who emails your editor on a weekly basis asking for an update. Depending on the length of the project per your contract, some editors may be OK with receiving an update request every other week. Other editors may be proactive about updating you on their progress. Still others may not contact you at all until they've finished your work.

If you're unclear about how often (or through which means) you should be contacting your editor, ask them about it before any work commences.

Editors all have their own specific ways of working and communicating with clients. While they should strive to serve clients as well as they can, editors often have certain processes in place in order to streamline their own work in order to offer more value to their clients.

When a new author/editor relationship begins, it's certainly a bit like dating: each person has to learn more about the other person, and neither person should be reticent to share what works best for them.

Again, you have to find the happy medium between nagging and trusting. You can't implicitly trust an editor until they've proven their worth to you. But neither should you constantly contact a new editor in fear that they won't get your job done on time. Trust that who they've marketed themselves to be is true, but also realize that it's your responsibility to assess whether that editor is ultimately helping or hindering your book.

3. Ask for more than what's been agreed upon.

Contracts are the most boring part of the writer/editor relationship, but they may also be the most important. It's essential to the health of your professional relationships with editors (and agents and publishers) that you read and understand your contracts. The contract lays out everything required of you and required of the editor.

When you fail to see an important point in a contract, don't sign the contract. Contact the editor and kindly ask why a specific point was missing. They may have forgotten about it, misunderstood your previous verbal agreement, or they may have assumed it was covered by a different part of the contract.

Furthermore, contracts outline what each party agrees to offer. For the author, this typically means:

- The day by which they will get their completed manuscript to the editor
- The amount of money they'll pay the editor
- The timeframe and method by which they'll pay

For the editor, this means

- An explicit statement of the type of editing and/or writing work they'll be doing to the author's manuscript
- The style guide to be used on the book
- The deadline by which they'll have their edits completed

Other details may also be included, like the author retaining rights to his or her book, the author not holding the editor responsible for whether or not the book sells, confidentiality regarding the book's content, and the editor's legal nature as a contractor and not an employee. But, an author should pay strict attention to the bullet points mentioned above. It's imperative to the success of your author/editor relationship that both parties completely agree on what the contract says from the very beginning of the relationship.

If the work isn't outlined in the contract, an editor is not obligated to do such work. So, if you ask an editor to complete your edits a week earlier than the contract states because you found a better launch date, you can expect one of two answers:

1. Sure, but it'll cost more.
2. I can't do that. I'm all booked out.

Neither of these answers are the best, especially for budget-minded authors. However, this issue can play out in a number of ways, like when an author might request a copyeditor to do light developmental edits, or write promotional copy, or edit a new conclusion. While editors understand that such instances happen, there may be issues far outside of their control as to how they can provide adequate help to an author who's requesting more than what's already been agreed upon.

As best as you can, try to stay within the bounds of your contract. Again, that's why it's so important for the contract to be fully understood and mutually agreed upon by both parties *before* any work begins. Some inescapable issues may occur, like an editor getting sick or an author needing to extend their payment period, and it's perfectly acceptable for either party to contact the other to let them know what's happening. Like any good relationship, the key is to communicate. As inflexible as editors are about the English language, they tend to be more flexible with clients whom they want to retain. Prove yourself to be one of those clients by knowing your contract and sticking to it.

4. Seek free book consulting.

Closely related to the last point, first-time authors or self-publishers may request more help from an editor in regard to the production and marketing of their book. If they know that their editor has trod the path to publishing before, they may naively believe that the editor will freely give of his or her time in order to answer their questions. This is a dangerous line to toe, as an author may believe that they're actually asking only one simple question, but they're unaware that a simple question about marketing or publishing often leads to many more questions.

Editors want to help your book succeed, but they also have a business to run. Like you, their time is money. While I'm not saying that it's always inappropriate to ask production and marketing questions of your editor, I am saying that you should certainly be wary of essentially seeking free book consulting from your editor. With as much free and inexpensive content that exists online through podcasts, blogs, and cheap ebooks about book marketing and publishing, you don't need to press your luck by seeking such answers from your editor. Either do the work yourself—I've included helpful resources in the Afterword—or specifically ask your editor if they'd be open to offering book consulting on an hourly paid basis. If they don't offer that kind of service, they may be able to refer you to someone who does.

As I need to remind myself and other authors over and over again, having written a book is only the beginning of the process. Creating a professional product and conducting effective book marketing are equally as important if you want your words to be read by more than just the people you know. While an editor may be able to answer a few questions to help you on your path to publishing, that's not their specific job. You're paying them to clean up your copy, not to sell your book, which leads nicely into the next point.

5. Place an undue selling burden on the editor.

I have yet to come across an author who has blamed an editor for poor sales, but the contract template I use includes an indemnification clause regarding the "whims and caprices of the publishing industry." In other words, the author agrees to hold the editor harmless if the final, edited manuscript fails to sell the way the author desires. This seems like a self-evident statement, that no one can know how well a book may sell, but it's an important notion for authors to understand.

Though I'm adamant about authors hiring editors and cover designers to help make their books shine, such an investment is no guarantee that a book will sell. In fact, it's not even a guarantee that such a book will recoup its editing and design costs.

For example, let's say you've written a 50,000-word nonfiction ebook you'll sell for $4.99 on Amazon. You spent $700 on a mid-level copyeditor and around $300 for a crowd-sourced cover design through 99designs.com. All told, you've spent $1000. Per Amazon's 2014 royalty payment schedule of 70 percent (to the author) for ebooks priced between $2.99 and $9.99, you'll make approximately $3.42 per sale. To recoup your investment, you'll need to sell 293 books.

Whether you like it or not, writers must be marketers these days. For the most part, an author can blame no one but himself or herself for the ultimate success of a book. When they begin blaming an editor for poor sales, such an author is most likely looking for the nearest scapegoat. Book sales are dependent on such a vast array of factors that to blame any single issue is folly. Book sales occur for all of these reasons and more:

- Content
- Cover design
- Storytelling ability
- Platform
- Launch strategy
- Endorsements
- Marketing
- Timing
- Trends
- Dumb luck

The smart book marketer tries to discover workable solutions for each of the issues listed above. Instead of complaining about low book sales and seeking to blame anyone or anything else other than themselves or the work they've produced, smart authors are proactive. If they don't know about book marketing, they learn as much as they can. If they haven't built a platform, they join and engage in a social network where their fans already are. If they haven't sought endorsements from other respected authors, celebrities, or subject matter experts, they start asking for them. For help on book marketing, check out my recommended books in this book's Afterword, "20 Must-Read Books on Writing and Publishing."

As amazing or life-changing as your words may be, selling books today requires much more than just uploading your masterpiece to Amazon. If your book fails to sell the way you think it should, don't blame your editor, cover designer, agent, or publisher. Sure, part of your poor sales might actually be their fault, but as the author of the book, you're the one responsible for solving the problem. Don't complain; take control.

6. Disregard their suggestions.

For a moment, imagine yourself as the editor of someone else's book. Anxious to see the finished product, you buy the book the first day it's available. As soon as you receive it, you start reading, but right there on page seven, you spot a stray comma that you're certain you fixed. You go back to the original manuscript you edited to double-check yourself. Sure enough, you deleted that unnecessary comma—yet it still remains in the final published version, the book that says "Edited by You" on one of the front pages.

Sure, a vast majority of people won't care who edited a book. Name one editor of any book you've read in the last few months. But the lack of recognition editors receive from the reading public is an issue best saved for a whining blog post. The point I'm currently trying to make is that when a writer chooses to disregard his or her editor's suggestions, they run the risk of tarnishing the editor's reputation. Again, imagine yourself in their shoes. You've worked to make a book better, but the author chose to forego your well-intentioned suggestions for reasons unknown. Yet the author's decision could reflect poorly on your skills as an editor.

You can be sure that if you choose to disregard a majority of your editor's suggestions and still put their name on the finished product, that editor may find a number of reasons to not take on your next project.

Plus, why would you pay hundreds or thousands of dollars for an edit and not take an editor's advice? If you ever have a question about why an editor did something to your manuscript, *ask them about it*. Send a short email with your question, but be sure to specifically reference the title of your book and the page number on which the confusing change occurs. Capable editors should be able to tell you exactly why they chose that particular option and give you firm, documented reasons for their decision. Not only does this clear up misunderstandings, but it will also help you become a better writer. Again, transparent communication by both parties is an essential aspect to any writer/editor relationship.

If you realize that an editor is *for* you and your book and not *against* you as a writer, you'll appreciate and incorporate their suggestions.

Now, I'm not saying you should automatically accept every suggestion an editor makes. They're human, so they make mistakes as well. Once you receive your edits back, you should be meticulous in going through the edits one-by-one so you can ensure that your book is actually getting better because of an editor's help. You may have a character whose speech patterns dictate unique punctuation, and your editor may have tried to standardize the punctuation without asking you about it beforehand. Good editors will pick up on such issues though, especially if they're repeated throughout a text, and they will contact you about those seeming problems before proceeding with editing your book.

7. Take it personally.

This may be the most difficult issue to deal with when it comes to being edited. In fact, Chapter 6 covers our deep desire for validation as writers. (I purposefully say "our" too.) The worst thing an author can do after receiving their edits back is to take the editor's well-meaning suggestions as a sign that they should stop writing forever. No one wants to see the manuscript they've spent untold hours working on torn to shreds, bleeding under the innumerable slashes of a red pen. Word's Track Changes feature highlights problems in red as well, so there's no escaping seeing your book effectively murdered, even if you're using digital tools. (If you'd like to change the color to something less critical and murder-y, learn how at blke.co/16TK9L6.)

Seeing your book for the first time following an intense edit can be heart-breaking depending on your view of yourself as a writer. This holds especially true for first-time writers who have yet to share their works with writing professionals. But you can't allow editors' well-intentioned suggestions to deter you from becoming a better writer. In fact, you should view their edits as teachable moments. All writers have areas of weakness, and we will never become aware of them if other writers and editors don't graciously yet honestly point them out to us. Plus, it's much, much better to have a paid editor tell you about your writing deficiencies in private than to see those same remarks put into an eternal public record through negative online book reviews.

When a writer takes an editor's suggestions personally, it proves the writer to either be immature or arrogant. Immature writers may simply be ignorant of style guides and the basics of storytelling, or they may just not be well read. Consequently, such writers may be more prone to sending half-baked books that result in a large number of edits, causing the writer to take such edits as a sign they should quit writing altogether. This shouldn't be the case, as the only way for an immature writer to mature is to endure the welts that all successful writers later wear with pride.

On the other end of the spectrum, arrogant writers may think so highly of themselves or their craft that they consider themselves above editing. If they do in fact seek an editor's help, they may push back against every suggestion, arguing for fewer changes because "the work is already as good as it's going to get." This is literary hubris to the highest degree.

Everyone needs an editor.

Writers are far too close to their own works to ever be able to obtain an objective view of their books. It's not that anyone else can offer a purely objective view of a book, but an emotionally disconnected editor will be able to spot issues a writer—and especially an arrogant writer—can't see. When an over-confident writer receives edits back, they may take the suggestions personally and decide to incorporate none of the edits, a waste of both the author and the editor's time. Rather, such an author should practice humility (an essential posture for writers) and see the writer/editor relationship as a learning opportunity.

In many ways, the immature writer and the arrogant writer are much alike. They both need to mature as writers by learning that validation doesn't come from a flawless manuscript, a topic we'll cover in-depth in Chapter 6.

But before we get to that, let's look at one more issue that plagues writers: the epidemic of hurry.

5

LESS THAN READY

Words of Warning about Undercooked Books

"Too many struggling writers never suspect that the creation of a fine screenplay is as difficult as the creation of a symphony, and in some ways more so."
— Robert McKee, Story

I hate cooking. I thoroughly enjoy the results of cooking, but I hate cooking.

I'm impressed by those that do it well, but all of my attempts at cooking are in vain. I'm too impatient with the process and often too crestfallen with the results. Rationally, I know that my impatience is what leads to disastrous outcomes, but even knowing that doesn't make me want to get into the kitchen again and try harder or wait longer.

Let's just get honest: I want to eat good food, but I don't want to put the work into making good food. I will settle for quite the sub-par frozen dinner if it means I'm eating within five minutes of feeling hungry. This is not healthy physically, emotionally, or mentally, but it's the rut I've gotten myself into as a result of my own laziness and desire for comfort.

And comfort has much to do with my (lack of) cooking. Beyond wanting to eat as soon as possible, I also don't want to spend precious hours on preparing food that will just be consumed in thirty minutes or less. I have better things to do with my time. When two meal preparation options are presented to me and one requires significantly less time invested, that choice almost always wins, regardless of what type of food may be presented. A sumptuous rack of ribs versus a gray, meat-like substance wallowing in watered-down maybe-gravy? If I can have the latter cooked in a minute and eaten in three, I'll choose that. If I really want ribs, I'll pay someone else to make them for me. At least then I can eat their bread while waiting on dinner.

I don't like this about myself. It's a lifestyle choice that needs to change for a host of reasons I won't bore you with, but my story ought to be instructive for every author (myself included). Although I'm not assuming this is the case for a majority of writers, I've also read enough to know that there are likely thousands of books released every year that could have done better had they stayed in the oven longer.

In his *Journal of a Novel*, Steinbeck lays bare my cooking metaphor: "You can't train for something all your life and then have it fall short because you are hurrying to get it finished."

The Rush to Publish

It's my fear that the astounding ease-of-access self-publishing has granted to all writers has caused us to go mad with hurry. We rush "product" out of our digital doors and into the wide arms of the waiting world so we can validate ourselves as writers. We go from manuscript to published book without a single other soul having read our words—one of the most dangerous games you can play when it comes to publishing. We write and write and write, thinking we're telling a compelling story, yet we fail to realize that the only reason the story is compelling is because it's *our* story. We refrain from letting those close to us read our words for fear that they'll reject us in some way, but we have no qualms about releasing our words to the wider, faceless public.

Publishing a book isn't blogging. There's a certain ephemeral nature to blogging, where today's fresh content often trumps yesterday's stale, day-old bread. Yet a book is effectively forever. Yes, a blog post can remain online for as long as online exists, but it doesn't have the same kind of ongoing existence a book can have. You can always delete a blog post, but Amazon reviews are forever. I fear that the common way writers approach blogging is the same way that many approach creating a book. In fact, there are a number of books about blogging your book. I'm not necessarily saying that blogging a book is a bad idea, but I am admonishing all writers to lean into writing their books with the same kind of care, craftsmanship, and patience that a world-class chef might take with one of their more complex dishes.

I love the way screenwriting guru and writing coach Robert McKee says it: "Secure writers don't sell first drafts. They patiently rewrite until the script is as director-ready, as actor-ready as possible. Unfinished work invites tampering, while polished, mature work seals its integrity." In other words, readers quickly spot holes in the armor of unpolished work, but a completed book written by a patient author holds resolute. It may not be a perfect book, and it may not resonate with a wide number of readers, but for that author's true 1,000 fans, the book stands firm because its foundation has been patiently poured.

McKee goes on to say, "Given the choice between trivial material brilliantly told versus profound material badly told, an audience will always choose the trivial told brilliantly." When a writer makes an effective use of their time to properly build their book, they can make even the most mundane seem sublime simply by the art of their craft. Sometimes finding the right word may take days, months, or even years. Sometimes a book requires its author to live a little longer before unlocking itself for the author. Sometimes, as Austin Kleon writes, "Creative people need time to just sit around and do nothing."

The Impossible Path to Perfection

Have you noticed how sometimes your greatest plot ideas or turns of phrase come to you in the shower, or right before you finally drift into sleep? (Reasons 9 and 10 to always keep something near you on which to write). This occurs because your brain continues to work out possible solutions to your problems, even when you're not consciously considering those issues.

You can liken it to the fact that readers love resolution. Why? Because we're wired that way. When faced with insurmountable problems, we want resolution. We want answers to our quandaries. It's why we can't quit asking why we exist, or what our purpose is, or what's for dinner. From the spiritual to the corporeal, we constantly swim upstream in a river of questions, seeking fleeting answers like salmon jumping to mate. As in life, so too in writing: sometimes the answers we need require time more than anything else. That's one of the reasons why self-editing tip #1 is to rest your manuscript. Time may heal all wounds, but it's a beneficial salve for words too.

Yet there's a frightening stall tactic when it comes to giving too much time to your manuscript: the impossible drive for perfection. To paraphrase Ecclesiastes, "There's a time to mourn and a time to dance, a time to write and a time to ship." Books should be written with care minus the pressure of time, but they should also have a realistic deadline for publication. After all, if you're looking to make a career from your words, what's the point of writing?

Anne Lamott speaks to writers' penchants for seeking perfection:

> Perfectionism is the voice of the oppressor, the enemy of the people. It will keep you cramped and insane your whole life, and it is the main obstacle between you and a shitty first draft. I think perfectionism is based on the obsessive belief that if you run carefully enough, hitting each stepping-stone just right, you won't have to die. The truth is that you will die anyway and that a lot of people who aren't even looking at their feet are going to do a whole lot better than you, and have a lot more fun while they're doing it.

If you think about it, Lamott's telling you what I've told you from page one: don't fear the reaper. "The truth is you will die anyway." Those are harsh words, but the truth doesn't care about your feelings. The reality of your finite existence on earth should spur you to create. Considering that what you write could very well live on after you die, or even financially provide for your offspring, whether in a small or very noticeable way, is a fascinating motivator for producing quality work.

A caveat: I'm not completely against writers who espouse quick production timelines. Deadlines are essential to my work, and I encourage all authors to set deadlines of their own when faced with a daunting project. Such a deadline can be completely meaningless so long as it's firm. With a deadline on the calendar, setting daily writing goals becomes simple, and achieving those goals becomes a daily reassurance of proving to yourself that you're a writer.

In one of my favorite *Calvin & Hobbes* comic strips, Calvin teaches his real (stuffed) tiger the brutal truth located at the intersection of homework and procrastination:

Calvin: "You can't just turn on creativity like a faucet. You have to be in the right mood."
Hobbes: "What mood is that?"
Calvin: "Last-minute panic."

As you've read, fear of failure is a great motivator, but it's definitely not the right kind of motivator. Deadlines help you ship and place a perfection-killing preventative measure in front of you. Your deadline should motivate you to start your project *on the day you set your deadline* and *not* on Calvin's favorite day to complete his homework—the day before it's due.

Yet you may have read a book or a blog post that promises proven strategies to write thousands of words in a hour, or how to write a novel in ninety days. These efforts can be helpful for first drafts, but I fear that a well-defined distinction hasn't been made between quickly writing a first draft and the rest of the editing and publishing process, which can be slower than the writing itself, but is just as important.

Dozens of successful self-published authors became that way because they produced massive amounts of words in short amounts of time. I fear that we as authors do what most creatives tend to do: we compare our middle to someone else's end. In other words, we look at these authors' wild successes and desire to emulate that, so we errantly believe that just cranking out book after book after book is the way to go. But we don't know the full picture of the actual work that these authors have put into their books over a long period of time.

If I had to hazard a guess, these rapid writers weren't so rapid on their first book, or even on their third book. Yet as they practiced writing and publishing, they discovered ways to make more effective uses of their time. They may have learned to produce more words by paying others to take care of what they once did for themselves. They may have leveraged their growing fanbases to elicit immediate reader feedback, an invaluable and cheap form of developmental editing. Whatever strategies they may have developed over time, what I'm trying to get at is that it's OK to write fast, especially if it's your first draft, but I caution all writers—and especially first-time, self-publishing authors—to take their time when pursuing next steps after a first draft.

- Know what kind of editor would most benefit your book, then connect with that editor. Give them the time they need to do the best work they can on your book.
- If necessary, teach yourself proper formatting, or find a company or person who can help you make a professional-looking book. Though I have not used them, BookBaby.com seems to offer an affordable and expansive package for getting your book formatted for a wide variety of digital formats, as well as print.
- If self-publishing, pay for a cover design. *Pay for a cover design.* ***Pay for a cover design.***

- Give a digital copy of your book for free to one-hundred beta readers. Ask for their honest reviews on launch day. Expect 10 percent to follow through, but be thrilled with that 10 percent. Every review helps, even the poor and middling ones, so long as the positive reviews outweigh the negative.

Yes, your book may not earn back your investment in an editor, formatting, and cover design, but by investing into those particular aspects of your book, you're offering the world your most polished work and cementing yourself as a professional writer intent on producing more and better work in the future.

Your book doesn't have to be a masterpiece so long as it's an honest effort on your part to produce something that helps or entertains another person. Your book doesn't have to be perfect (everyone needs an editor), but it should be produced with patient professionalism. Your book doesn't have to be written in thirty days, ninety days, or five years. However long it takes to write a polished version of your book is how long it will take you to write a polished version of your book.

I wish I could tell you a formula so you could know when your book is ready for an editor or beta readers, but one doesn't exist. It's just something you'll feel the more often you arrive at that threshold.

Also, there's no shame in asking trusted writer connections for their opinions on the readiness of your book. Seek out authors who have crossed that threshold many times before and ask for their honest, no-holding-back, no-hurt-feelings opinion. Give careful consideration to their words, but realize that you are still the tiny god of your own literary kingdom. You have the final say; just be sure that your final say is said at the exact moment before you overwork your manuscript in a vain striving for perfection. Even with all the professional help in the world, your book will not be perfect.

Now that you have that proverbial monkey off of your shoulders, you can walk freely into any pitch to an agent or editor, knowing your book might have its flaws, but confident in its patient construction and honest reflection of your perspective on life, the universe, and everything.

As you write today, be free from the tyranny of the rushed. Give yourself and your book breathing room. While you're waiting, maybe go cook something.

The kitchen's a fine place to learn how to write.

6

UNVEILING VALIDATION'S HIDING PLACE

How to Defeat Every Writer's Nightmare

"Even if I knew nothing
would emerge from this book I would still write it."
— John Steinbeck on *East of Eden*

Validation is a loaded word. It's not something that's discussed in polite company, and a group of writers would likely rather talk about anything else than disclose their need for validation to one another.

To make matters worse, validation has wildly different origins from one writer to the next. Yet validation was the first word that came to my mind when I considered writing this short book.

Maybe that says more about me than it does you, but I believe validation to be a deep desire for all writers, sometimes so clouded in the hundreds of details of writing, publishing, and marketing a book that we have trouble discovering why we're frustrated with our book's progress or reception. We want to be known as good writers, but far too often we look to the wrong indicators to validate our writing lives.

In this chapter, you'll hear from dozens of respected authors. While some of these thoughts on validation are my own, a majority of them come from the written words of known authors who have long trod the path of the writing life. This chapter is meant as both a diagnosis and a cure—if a cure for writers' validation could be found.

By the time you've finished this comparatively lengthy chapter, it's my hope that you'd be able to detect where you've vainly searched for validation and reorient your writing life so that the validation you long for is properly sought, achieved, and funneled back into your writing career.

By and large, the issues I list aren't bad in and of themselves, but whenever they become the ultimate arbiter of your "writerliness," they assume the power to destroy your confidence—and that's one characteristic a writer can't do without.

Validation Means Wanting to Be Known

If I had to hazard a guess, writers since the dawn of time have struggled with validation. I'm willing to bet that the artist who created the cave paintings at Lascaux wondered if anyone would ever care about his or her drawings. Did the artist paint to document history, to impress a significant other, or just because he or she was bored? (Maybe the painter was just waiting on dinner to be cooked.) Even if that ancient artist may not have been aware of it, his or her work indicated a deep need to be known.

In *On Writing*, his must-read book for writers, Stephen King said,

> Writing isn't about making money, getting famous, getting dates, getting laid, or making friends. In the end, it's about enriching the lives of those who will read your work, and enriching your own life, as well. It's about getting up, getting well, and getting over. Getting happy, okay? Getting happy.

Do you believe that?

In *Walking on Water*, Madeline L'Engle says that "to paint a picture or to write a story or to compose a song is an incarnational activity." When we create, whether through words, painting, music, or some other avenue, we give part of ourselves to the world. We "incarnate," or bring life to, something that only existed in our minds.

Stop and think about that incredible aspect of the writing life: what once was only in your mind now exists in the real world.

L'engle goes on to illustrate the writer's response to their inner drive:

> The artist must be obedient to the work, whether it be a symphony, a painting, or a story for a small child. I believe that each work of art, whether it is a work of great genius, or something very small, comes to the artist and says, 'Here I am. Enflesh me. Give birth to me.' And the artist either says, 'My soul doth magnify the Lord,' and willingly becomes the bearer of the work, or refuses.

Writing a book is an intensely personal process. We pour our minds and souls into our words. When we release those words to an editor and then to the world at large, it's as if we're sending our firstborn off to college. They might be harassed, ridiculed, and criticized, and our emotional closeness to them makes us feel the full brunt of their pain. We want to defend them against the ways of the world, but we have to trust that what we've poured into them will win out in the end.

John Steinbeck coddled his works-in-progress like a mother hen her chicks. After completing the writing on *East of Eden*, he wrote in *Journal of a Novel*, "The book is done. It has no virtue any more. The writer wants to cry out—'Bring it back! Let me rewrite it or better—Let me burn it. Don't let it out in the unfriendly cold in that condition."

Yet the world can be as equally gracious, accepting, and kind as it can be critical. I tend to assume that many writers have a glass-half-empty perspective on their work, meaning that they might be insecure about their words despite working as hard as they can to hide their doubts. It's why artists sometimes seem starved for validation—whether they admit to it or not. When we create something real from just the thoughts in our minds, there's a deep yet subtle need for us to seek validation for that creation. We desire someone's "Good job" just to let us know our work was worth the effort.

In Anne Lamott's contemporary classic on writing, *Bird by Bird*, she visualizes a writer's need for validation as almost an act of hubris: "This is what separates artists from ordinary people: the belief, deep in our hearts, that if we build our castles well enough, somehow the ocean won't wash them away. I think this is a wonderful kind of person to be."

I think this is why turning a book over to an editor can be challenging for a first-time author. They fear their sandcastles may be kicked over by a bully editor strolling down the beach. But it's the editor's job to tear down where necessary, in order for a better, more enduring sandcastle to take shape, one that can weather the constant, capricious, rolling waves of readers and reviewers.

Yet the writer may take such corrections as validation of their "unwriterliness." When the writer fails to hear "Good job" from an editor—who should know good writing from bad—the writer's need for positive validation hits the proverbial brick wall. They feel sand sting their eyes as they witness their castles fall into the sea.

In such instances, the writer may take one of two routes: stop writing altogether, or disregard the editor's suggestions and publish anyway as an attempt to prove their own "writerliness."

Neither path is helpful for a writer who wants to make a career out of writing.

What I'm trying to say is this: a writer should *never* look for validation from an editor. That's not an editor's job. An editor may *never* offer you encouragement. They may only point out where your manuscript is lacking, or where your comma usage is deplorable, or where your characters are more boring than drying paint.

While I believe that good editors *do* offer praise when it's warranted, that's not their job. You want to hire an editor that's not afraid to tell you the truth about your manuscript, but you have to be secure enough in your own writing that you can take their suggestions to heart and learn to grow through the experience. When you receive a manuscript back from an editor that's riddled in red, you must not see that as evidence you should stop writing. View it as a testimony to the fact that you're a professional writer seeking professional help so you can produce a professional piece of art.

Yet a writer's need for validation still exists, so where should it be sought?

Before getting to the positives, let's look at where we as writers far too often—and far too vainly—seek validation.

Seeking Validation from Readers

The most obvious area for a writer to seek validation is from his or her readers, but this can be treacherous. I'm as guilty as most any other author in refreshing my Amazon sales page far too many times on launch day (and the weeks and months thereafter). It's thrilling to see your numbers climb, or to read a new and glowing review of the book you worked so hard to write. There's a definite physical, mental, and emotional reaction that occurs when experiencing such affirming feedback. It's hard not to gloat about your successes on social media or in your real-world conversations. It's validation in the truest sense of the word. Your readers' positive reactions have validated your self-worth as a writer.

But there's a dangerous corollary to that. What if the book tanks? What if your initial reviews are less than stellar? What if social media twists your intentions? If you stake your "writerliness" on your readers' reception, you run the risk of becoming even more insecure as a writer if readers don't connect with the book. For the same high you feel with every five-star review, you'll feel an equal lowness (if not even more pronounced) with every one- or two-star review.

Not everyone will think your book is astounding, compelling, or the must-read novel of the year. Even the most famous of authors have their detractors, but they know better than to stake their need for validation on the whims and fancies of a mostly unknown readership. In *On Writing*, Stephen King wrote,

> I have spent a good many years—too many, I think—being ashamed about what I write. I think I was forty before I realized that almost every writer of fiction or poetry who has ever published a line has been accused by someone of wasting his or her

God-given talent. If you write (or paint or dance or sculpt or sing, I suppose), someone will try to make you feel lousy about it, that's all.

Steinbeck opted for patience when it came to allowing his words to find the right kinds of readers:

> [*East of Eden*] will not be what anyone expects and so the expecters will not like it. And until it gets to people who don't expect anything and are just willing to go along with the story, no one is likely to like this book.

In *The War of Art*, Steven Pressfield gets straight to the harsh truth about the writing life and waiting for positive public reception:

> The artist committing himself to his calling has volunteered for hell, whether he knows it or not. He will be dining for the duration on a diet of isolation, rejection, self-doubt, despair, ridicule, contempt, and humiliation.

Are you ready for that kind of dinner?

This is the point where you may be asking yourself, "Is this kind of work really for me?" Pressfield understands:

> If you find yourself asking yourself (and your friends), "Am I really a writer? Am I really an artist?" chances are you are. The counterfeit innovator is wildly self-confident. The real one is scared to death.

If you're scared to death of releasing your words, keep reading.

It gets worse.

Seeking Validation from Income

In the film *Get Shorty*, Harry Zimm succinctly summarizes the writer's monetary plight: "I once asked this literary agent what kind of writing paid the best. He said, 'Ransom notes.'"

Never seek validation for your writing based on the amount of money you receive in return for your words. A majority of indie authors who sell on Amazon don't make enough to financially support themselves. If you're pinning your retirement hopes on your first novel, you'd do better to buy yourself a book about writing. Of the authors who do make enough to write full-time, they typically have multiple books on sale, and they've been working arduously for years to get to that point. The chances of you earning a working wage during the first few years of your writing journey are slim to none. The sooner you can accept that fact, the sooner you'll be free from the shackles of absurd financial expectations.

Seeking financial validation is just as capricious as seeking reader validation. You'll ride a roller coaster of emotions until you puke depression and anxiety. Like a tired dog on a leash, your inner worth will always lag behind your last royalty report. The income that arrives as a result of your words should be seen as an added bonus. It's OK to feel validated for a moment by better sales, but never equate your worth as a writer with your royalty statement.

Pressfield paints a stark picture of one who seeks validation from income: "To labor in the arts for any reason other than love is prostitution."

Steinbeck understood that. "I am not writing for money any more now than I ever did. If money comes that is fine, but [if] I knew right now that this book would not sell a thousand copies, I would still write it."

Going back to Pressfield, he combines the two main validation impostors of other people and their money: "The artist cannot look to others to validate his efforts or his calling. If you don't believe me, ask Van Gogh, who produced masterpiece after masterpiece and never found a buyer in his whole life."

Not that I need to remind you, but Van Gogh's paintings are sold for millions today—millions that he never earned in his lifetime, and yet he continued to paint because he couldn't not paint.

Money and income are an important part of the equation for a long-lasting career in writing, but they shouldn't be used as sole barometers for your success.

Seeking Validation from Being a Writer

Like arguments over the Oxford comma, people will likewise disagree about what constitutes a "real" writer. Is it someone who:

- writes anything?
- journals in a diary?
- blogs?
- self-publishes?
- traditionally publishes?
- earns a living wage through writing?
- is a known-name author?

The mystique of the writer is a long-running trope, especially in America where authors of all kinds strive to write "The Great American Novel." As self-publishing begins to overtake traditional publishing, more and more writers are becoming authors, and there's an allure within this process of finally being able to call oneself a professional writer, even if the "gatekeepers" of traditional publishing have denied these authors' book proposals time and time again. The DIY model of self-publishing opens the floodgates of publishing, allowing all stripes of writers to offer their books to the world.

This is equally as bad as it is good. Though I have no research but my own assumptions to back this up, I'd guess that for every one hundred self-published books, one is worth reading. That might be charitable too, and this statement comes from a self-published author who's a fan of self-publishing.

An aside: there's still a small stigma attached to self-publishing, though it's lessening day-by-day. If you're ever in a conversation where you're made to feel comparatively small because you opted to self-publish, ask that person to name the publisher of the last book they read. Then, share with them the difference in royalty percentages between self-publishing and traditional publishing, which could be 70 percent for self-published authors and hover under 15 percent for traditionally published authors. The general public doesn't know about the quickly shifting tides in the publishing industry, and just a little bit of teaching can go a long way toward validating your self-published book in their eyes.

I believe that one of the drivers of drivel in self-publishing is a result of writers seeking validation from *being a writer.* If I can say to someone in the general public, "I have a book on Amazon," most people would think that's impressive, regardless of the quality of the book itself. There's cultural cachet in telling others, "I'm a writer." (Or maybe, as a writer, I just want there to be.)

But seeking validation through identifying as a writer can be maddening. Why? Because writers are among the most insecurely confident people on earth. Self-nullifying quotes about the writing life abound:

- "I hate writing. I love having written."— Dorothy Parker
- "I have great faith in fools. Self-confidence my friends call it. " — Edgar Allan Poe
- "I know it is the best book I have ever done. I don't know whether it is good enough." —John Steinbeck
- "I know some very great writers, writers you love who write beautifully and have made a great deal of money, and not one of them sits down routinely feeling wildly enthusiastic and confident. Not one of them writes elegant first drafts. All right, one of them does, but we do not like her very much." — Anne Lamott

- "No matter our talent, we all know in the midnight of our souls that 90 percent of what we do is less than our best." — Robert McKee

Steinbeck gets to the heart of the writer's dilemma:

> And the greatest foolishness of all lies in the fact that to do it at all, the writer must believe that what he is doing is the most important thing in the world. And he must hold to this illusion even when he knows it is not true. If he does not, the work is not worth even what it might otherwise have been.

Pressfield supposes why writers can be so fearful of their own work:

> We fear discovering that we are more than we think we are. More than our parents/children/teachers think we are. We fear that we actually possess the talent that our still, small voice tells us. That we actually have the guts, the perseverance, the capacity. We fear that we truly can steer our ship, plant our flag, reach our Promised Land. We fear this because, if it's true, then we become estranged from all we know. We pass through a membrane. We become monsters and monstrous.

Serious writers vacillate between wild self-confidence and deep insecurity. They must simultaneously believe that what they write is an important contribution to the world while also holding their book with an open hand, willing to suffer whatever slings and arrows the world volleys back at them. Staking your validation on being a writer can backfire as soon as the first negative review of your writing ability gets posted online, or in that first moment when you open your vastly edited manuscript.

You should absolutely take pride in being a writer, but you shouldn't singularly identify yourself that way. Again, Steinbeck offers invaluable advice on how to separate yourself from something that seems so much a part of yourself. "The book is a thing in itself, and it is not *me*. There is no ego in it. I am glad that you sense that while I am in it and of it, I am not the book. It is much more than I am."

I think one of the many things Steinbeck was getting at in that fascinating turn of phrase is the fact that books—if done well—are eternal. They are "much more" than their authors because books live on well after the author's own shelf-life has expired. Pressfield echoes the same sentiment: "The professional loves her work. She is invested in it wholeheartedly. But she does not forget that the work is not her." When you can separate yourself from your book, the flaming arrows of criticism will only scorch your shoulder instead of piercing your heart.

Where to Seek Validation as a Writer

When writers can remove their egos from the process—as much as they're able—their words will shine, since a veneer of "writerly" pretense hasn't been allowed to accumulate throughout the book. So how can a writer, who must be somewhat self-centered and vain in the first place to even be a writer, remove his or her ego from the process?

Consider the lake.

> If the work comes to the artist and says, 'Here I am, serve me,' then the job of the artist, great or small, is to serve. The amount of the artist's talent is not what it is about. Jean Rhys said to an interviewer in the Paris Review, 'Listen to me. All of writing is a huge lake. There are great rivers that feed the lake, like Tolstoy and Dostoyevsky. And there are mere trickles, like Jean Rhys. **All that matters is feeding the lake. I don't matter. The lake matters. You must keep feeding the lake**
> — Madeline L'engle, *Walking on Water*, emphasis added

In other words, the writing life demands that the writer be found writing. That's not profound, but it's a practical definition of what a writer ought to be doing. It reminds me of one of the most simple and oft-quoted lines from a modern cinematic classic. What encourages reticent intergalactic space pilots holds true for writers as well: "Do or do not. There is no try."

In *Steal Like an Artist*, Austin Kleon wrote, "It's in the act of making things and doing our work that we figure out who we are." But even then, we writers suffer from the fear of failure. We worry about public reception, critical reviews, and whether or not we're really worth our salt as writers. Still, as Pressfield goes on to say, "It's better to be in the arena, getting stomped by the bull, than to be up in the stands or out in the parking lot." If you don't believe that as a writer, your ego will be gored to death.

In Blake Snyder's *Save the Cat*, he contrasts the power of outside validation versus the power of internal motivation:

> The powers-that-be can take away a lot of things. They can buy your script and fire you, or rewrite it into oblivion, but they can't take away your ability to get up off the mat and come back swinging—better and smarter than you were before.

Steinbeck considers writers from the perspective of those who will never write: "And in the fullness of their [non-writers'] days they die with none of the tearing pain of failure because having tried nothing they have not failed."

It's "do or do not" all over again.

Hugh MacLeod's *Ignore Everybody And 39 Other Keys to Creativity* offers the same refrain:

> Doing something seriously creative is one of the most amazing experiences one can have .... If you can pull it off, it's worth it. Even if you don't end up pulling it off, you'll learn many incredible, magical, valuable things. It's not doing it—when you know full well you had the opportunity—that hurts far more than any failure.
>
> Frankly, I think you're better off doing something on the assumption that you will *not* be rewarded for it, that it will *not* receive the recognition it deserves, that it will *not* be worth the time and effort invested in it.
>
> The obvious advantage to this angle is, of course, if anything good comes of it, then it's an added bonus.
>
> The second, more subtle and profound advantage is that by scuppering all hope of worldly and social betterment from the creative act, you are finally left with only one question to answer:
>
> Do you make this damn thing exist or not?
>
> And once you can answer that truthfully for yourself, the rest is easy.

You should be noticing a trend by now.

Pressfield says, "We must do our work for its own sake, not for fortune or attention or applause." If you can be honest to yourself about yourself and affirm your disinterest in the world's affirmation, there's still a more challenging question to ask yourself if you want to know how serious you are about being a writer. Pressfield asks it: "Of any activity you do, ask yourself: If I were the last person on earth, would I still do it?"

In the same vein, Madeline L'engle quotes Rainer Maria Rilke's *Letters to a Young Poet*:

> You are looking outward, and that above all you should not do now. Nobody can counsel and help you, nobody. There is only one single way. Go into yourself. Search for the reason that bids you to write; find out whether it is spreading out its roots in the deepest places of your heart, acknowledge to yourself whether you would have to die if it were denied you to write. This above all—ask yourself in the stillest hour of your night: *Must* I write? Delve into yourself for a deep answer. And if this should be affirmative, if you may meet this earnest question with a strong and simple 'I must,' then build your life according to this necessity; your life even into its most indifferent and slightest hour must be a sign of this urge and testimony to it.

For some writers, the question of "Must I write?" has already been answered. For others, they may need to take some time to give serious consideration to that probing question. There are a thousand variations of this question, all of which focus on validation:

- If I never made a dollar from my writing, would I still write?
- If I never received a positive review, would I still write?
- If this was the only book I ever released, would I still write?
- If no publishers wanted my book, would I still write?
- If everyone in my life believes my writing to be a waste of time, would I still write?

Note that all of these hypothetical questions concern what happens *after* the writing's been finished. Steinbeck reveals what many experienced authors know: it's not about the result; it's about the process. When he was headlong and knee-deep into writing *East of Eden*, he wrote, "This is a time of great joy. It will never be so good again—never. A book finished, published, read—is always an anticlimax to me. The joy comes in the words going down and the rhythms crowding in the chest and pulsing to get out."

Anne Lamott phrases the "Should I write?" question so well. "This business of becoming conscious, of being a writer, is ultimately about asking yourself, 'How alive am I willing to be?'" Not that I need to remind you, but part of being alive means doing work, and *it's in doing the work of the writer that you will find validation as a writer.*

In Austin Kleon's excellent *Steal Like an Artist*, within the perfectly titled subchapter "Validation Is for Parking," he writes,

> The trouble with creative work: Sometimes by the time people catch on to what's valuable about what you do, you're either a) bored to death with it, or b) dead. You can't go looking for validation from external sources. Once you put your work into the world, you have no control over the way people will react to it.
>
> Ironically, really good work often appears to be effortless. People will say, 'Why didn't I think of that?' They won't see the years of toil and sweat that went into it.
>
> Not everybody will get it. People will misinterpret you and what you do. They might even call you names. So get comfortable with being misunderstood, disparaged, or ignored—**the trick is to be too busy doing your work to care** (emphasis added).

Stephen King knows about being found busy and disregarding outside validation:

> When you find something at which you are talented, you do it (whatever it is) until your fingers bleed or your eyes are ready to fall out of your head. Even when no one is listening (or reading, or watching), every outing is a bravura performance, because you as the creator are happy. Perhaps even ecstatic.

In what may be the most succinct summation of this chapter, Hugh MacLeod wrote, "The best way to get approval is not to need it."

When you're too busy doing your work to care about public reception, you'll have arrived at the point where you don't need external approval. That small and quiet voice inside should be reminding you—as you work on your writing—that **the creative act of writing itself ought to be validation enough**.

Plus, when you're able to write without forcing your words to seek the approval of others, whether that's friends and family, literary critics, or the general public, your words will take on a much greater depth. They will reflect you in a much better light than if they were written as a way to seek validation from others. As much as you must work to separate yourself from your words upon public release, they must remain close to you during the writing itself—so close that every word you type ought to be a breath. It is within such personal work that you will find validation of a different and higher sort, and any positives that may later occur because of your words can be considered as gracious gifts given to an ardent worker.

It's one of the mysteries of the writing life: a writer must be egotistical enough to believe that their writing has meaning, but humble enough to present it to the world without the need for external validation. Money, fame, and talent ebb and flow. That's why looking to any of those as signifiers of having "made it" as a writer is worthless.

For what it's worth, writers never "make it." They just edge a bit closer with every word they write. The writing life is lifetime choice, a heeding of a persistent call, a bowing to the internal command: *write!* A writer writes because they *can't not* write. They don't do it for the royalties, the renown, or the reviews. They do it for the same reason that any person does anything they're passionate about: the love of the work itself.

Anne Lamott likens writing to hoping:

> I heard a preacher say recently that hope is a revolutionary patience; let me add that so is being a writer. Hope begins in the dark, the stubborn hope that if you just show up and try to do the right thing, the dawn will come. You wait and watch and work: you don't give up.

You can hope for positive public reception, glowing reviews, raving fans, and large royalty checks—all good things—but it's doing the work that proves the worker true. As you write, you validate *yourself* as a writer. With every new word you type, every old word you edit, and every new book you publish, you declare your "writerliness." You feed the lake and in turn the lake feeds you. You don't need external validation because you're too busy working on the next book, too busy becoming a better writer, and too focused on your craft to care about circumstances beyond your control that shouldn't dictate your worth as a writer.

Validation as a writer comes *through the work*, not because of it. Validation comes long before the world at large knows you've written a book. Validation comes because you're doing the work you were created to do.

In one of my favorite passages from Pressfield's *War of Art*, he echoes Yoda's wise "Do or do not" mantra:

> Are you a born writer? Were you put on earth to be a painter, a scientist, an apostle of peace? In the end the question can only be answered by action.
>
> Do it or don't do it.
>
> It may help to think of it this way. If you were meant to cure cancer or write a symphony or crack cold fusion and you don't do it, you not only

> hurt yourself, even destroy yourself. You hurt your children. You hurt me. You hurt the planet.
>
> You shame the angels who watch over you and you spite the Almighty, who created you and only you with your unique gifts, for the sole purpose of nudging the human race one millimeter farther along its path back to God.
>
> **Creative work is not a selfish act or a bid for attention on the part of the actor. It's a gift to the world and every being in it. Don't cheat us of your contribution. Give us what you've got** (emphasis added).

If you're not inspired to start writing right now, you may want to consider another line of work.

Today, let tomorrow worry about itself. Instead, go and do the good work of writing you've been called to do. Find validation in the act of writing itself, then be open to accepting whatever the world may send your way as a result of your words.

By giving us what you've got, you validate yourself as a writer.

AFTERWORD

20 Must-Read Books on Writing and Publishing

I can get lost in reading books about writing.

They're often the perfect way to get away from the hard work of writing while still feeling like you're working on your writing. That's not to denigrate these fine books; it's meant to serve as a word of warning.

If you're a writer, you may enjoy reading about writing and other writers' processes, but don't let these books became an escape from the work you're meant to be doing. Definitely take time to read these books, as I firmly believe they will help you become a better writer, but don't fool yourself into thinking that such reading is the work you should be doing as a writer. Consider setting aside thirty minutes to an hour of your day to read through these books, but never let them trump the time you've set aside for actual writing.

To Edit Well

The following books are listed in order of helpfulness when it comes to creating work that's ready for an editor.

1. *Grammar Girl's Quick and Dirty Tips for Better Writing*

blke.co/1zUQyhW

"Are you stumped by split infinitives?
Terrified of using 'who' when 'whom' is called for?
Do you avoid the words 'affect' and 'effect' altogether?"
— Mignon Fogarty

By the straightforward title, you should know what to expect from Mignon Fogarty's book. She covers just about every confusing aspect of grammar, punctuation, capitalization, usage, and more. It's an accessible book that's easy to read, as well as a quick reference guide you can pick up when you run into a thorny grammar situation.

The first chapter covers the most commonly troublesome words, like affect vs. effect and less vs. fewer, and includes helpful examples throughout the text. The remaining chapters offer quick, keen advice on proper usage and grammar, and she's smart about noting when a rule is a rule or when it's simply a style choice that multiple authorities disagree on (like ending a sentence with a preposition).

Fogarty's book is an extension of her popular (and highly recommended) Grammar Girl podcast (www.quickanddirtytips.com/grammar-girl), a short, daily podcast that offers one or two "quick and dirty" tips for better writing.

2. *The Elements of Style*

blke.co/1Fnp5sy

"Never call a stomach a tummy without good reason."
— Strunk and White

Time Magazine named Strunk and White's slim, classic, acerbic volume one of the one hundred most influential nonfiction books of the twentieth century. Cornell professor William Strunk Jr. self-published the book in 1918 for his students, but it wasn't until E.B. White (of *Charlotte's Web* fame) revised the book in 1959 that it became the behemoth (in terms of influence, not pages) of style and usage.

Elements lives up to its name by somehow distilling the vast intricacies of the English language to eight rules of usage, ten principles of composition, some words regarding form, forty-nine commonly misused words and phrases, and fifty-seven troublesome words to spell.

Elements is a useful starting place for neophyte grammarians, but you don't have to take it as gospel-truth. Like most style guides, it offers suggestions that create a baseline of standardization for proper English usage, yet these hard-and-fast rules can be broken, but only when the writing demands it.

Until you've written a million words or so, I'd recommend sticking with their suggestions. You should know the rules inside out before daring to break any of them.

3. *The Chicago Manual of Style, 16th Edition*

blke.co/1vJVwj1

"The indispensable reference for all who work with words."

If you really want to present as clean of a manuscript as possible to your editor, you'll buy and learn how to use *The Chicago Manual of Style* (CMOS). This is the Bible of the publishing industry, the style guide that outlines almost every aspect of grammar, usage, punctuation, style, and more.

If you're writing a book, this is the resource your editor will be using in order to make corrections. They may even cite particular chapters and sections (e.g., CMOS 8.1) when editing so you can verify whether the edits are merited. For instances where the CMOS does not specifically cover an issue, they offer a helpful forum (www.chicagomanualofstyle.org/forum.html) and the Chicago Style Q&A (www.chicagomanualofstyle.org/qanda/latest.html). Note that some sections of their website are only accessible to paid subscribers.

All writers should become familiar with *The Chicago Manual of Style*, as it will help them become technically better writers. You can either purchase the large print edition (blke.co/1vJVwj1) or a yearly subscription to the online version for $35 per year (www.chicagomanualofstyle.org/subscription_opts.html). I prefer the online edition as it allows me to quickly locate answers.

4. *On Writing*

blke.co/11sMhXf

"Write with the door closed, rewrite with the door open."
— Stephen King

Stephen King's contemporary classic *On Writing* is a must-have for any serious writer. Whether you appreciate his style or not, there's no escaping the fact that he's sold hundreds of millions of books over his long career. He knows how to write clearly and how to engage an audience.

Flowing from memoir to craft advice and back again, *On Writing* pulls back the curtain on King's process, his hatred of adverbs ("The road to hell is paved with adverbs."), and his ruminations on how to write compelling stories. "When the reader hears strong echoes of his or her own life and beliefs, he or she is apt to become more invested in the story."

Some of the advice may seem self-evident to longtime readers or writers, but for budding writers, such insider information is gold, especially as they begin to see how every small suggestion builds upon the last until a clear and compelling story is being told using narrative techniques that have proven themselves for ages.

5. *On Writing Well*

blke.co/1xSjkAW

"Clutter is the disease of American writing. We are a society strangling in unnecessary words, circular constructions, pompous frills and meaningless jargon."
— William Zinsser

Sadly, William Zinsser is as correct today as he was in 1976. Fortunately, his now-classic writing book works to offset the malady that plagues our magazines, blogs, emails, and books.

On Writing Well is a must-read for nonfiction authors. (Considering that fiction authors are encouraged to blog, which often takes the form of nonfiction writing, I recommend it for fiction writers as well.) His opening chapters on simplicity and clutter cut to the heart of good writing, as well as how to make your book as ready as possible for an editor. "Writing improves in direct ratio to the number of things we can keep out of it that shouldn't be there." Later, Zinsser shares a line that may thrill you or make you cringe: "Most first drafts can be cut by 50 percent without losing any information or losing the author's voice."

Zinsser's book is straightforward, and he offers advice to make your writing likewise straightforward-yet-personal. Though first released in 1976, *On Writing Well* is a perennial bestseller, and with good reason.

To Tell a Better Story

The following books won't help you write a technically better book, but they will greatly assist you with the basics of storytelling.

1. *Story: Style, Structure, Substance, and the Principles of Screenwriting*

blke.co/15nFh08

"True character is revealed in the choices a human being makes under pressure—the greater the pressure, the deeper the revelation, the truer the choice to the character's essential nature."
— Robert McKee

If you've ever seen *Adaptation* starring Nicholas Cage, you know this book. Screenwriting guru Robert McKee is depicted in that film as a cantankerous, foul-mouthed writing teacher, full of lines like, "Any idiot can write a voiceover narration to explain the thoughts of a character," spoken in the middle of a voiceover within the film.

McKee took his decades of highly sought after writing conferences and condensed them into a lengthy tome on the epitome of story, covering every aspect that makes a story compelling and consequently, one would hope, revenue-producing.

Story is not an easy read because of the wealth of information McKee provides, but I can guarantee you that it's a worthwhile read.

2. *Save the Cat!*

blke.co/1FnpRpi

"The 'Save the Cat' scene is where we meet the hero and the hero does something—like saving a cat—that defines who he is and makes us, the audience, like him."
— Blake Snyder

This modern classic on screenwriting shows how a story template (or "beats") can be laid over just about any movie in existence. It's helpful to see how the plots to hundreds of different movies can be boiled down to a few essentials, both providing fodder for your own stories as well as helping you to dissect any movies (or written narratives) you consume in the future.

Furthermore, his opening chapter on devising a logline for your script (i.e., an enticing one-sentence description) is imminently helpful for all writers looking to pitch their books to editors, agents, or reviewers.

As you've noticed, the first two books in this section mainly focus on screenwriting. While writing a script is very different from writing a book, authors would do well to learn what they can from the world of film when it concerns their storytelling abilities.

3. *The Hero with a Thousand Faces*

blke.co/1ANSDj3

"The latest incarnation of Oedipus, the continued romance of Beauty and the Beast, stand this afternoon on the corner of 42nd Street and Fifth Avenue, waiting for the traffic light to change."
— Joseph Campbell

Save the Cat digs into character archetypes, but it's a shallow offering considering Joseph Campbell's epic *The Hero with a Thousand Faces.*

If you really want to dig into the mythology of character archetypes and write using "the hero's journey" as your guide, you'll want to read Campbell's influential book on telling compelling stories. He taps into humanity's longest-lasting storytelling tropes, those ideas and characters we see time and time again throughout literature, and explains why these stories often resonate so deeply with so many.

This is the most academic and challenging book to read on this list.

4. *How to Write a Novel Using the Snowflake Method*

blke.co/1CaBKkc

"You're going to get lots of advice on how to write a novel. But that's all it is. Advice. If you don't like that advice, if it doesn't work for you, then ignore it. If it does work for you, then run with it."
— Randy Ingermason

How to Write a Novel Using the Snowflake Method offers a prescriptive method for composing a story. Told as a story itself, the presentation is whimsical, featuring Goldilocks as a struggling writer-to-be who thinks she has a good story to tell, but isn't sure how to go about writing an entire book. Her writing teacher, Baby Bear, presents her with "the snowflake method," essentially a way to outline your novel before digging into the lengthy work of writing it. The narrative of the book itself seeks to serve as an example of the method prescribed.

For writers with great stories whose minds go blank when confronted with a blank page, this method could be what clears your path to a completed manuscript.

5. *Reading Like a Writer: A Guide for People Who Love Books and for Those Who Want to Write Them*

blke.co/1vJWFXN

"All the elements of good writing depend on the writer's skill in choosing one word instead of another. And what grabs and keeps our interest has everything to do with those choices."

— Francine Prose

In *On Writing*, Stephen King said, "If you want to be a writer, you must do two things above all others: read a lot and write a lot. There's no way around these two things that I'm aware of, no shortcut."

Francine Prose's *Reading Like a Writer* combines King's suggestions, so that when you're reading excerpts from the greats, you're also learning the craft of writing and storytelling. The aptly named Prose looks at passages from a wide swath of literature (Dostoevsky, Austen, Kafka, Chekhov, Le Carré, et al.) to see both how their words affect the reader and why their words have endured.

To Be Inspired

These books are a constant inspiration to my writing. I've underlined dozens of quotes from each and return to these authors' words often, especially when my inner critic starts becoming too vocal.

1. *The War of Art: Break Through the Blocks and Win Your Inner Creative Battles*

blke.co/1rbjX80

"Are you paralyzed with fear? That's a good sign. Fear is good. Like self-doubt, fear is an indicator. Fear tells us what we have to do. Remember one rule of thumb: the more scared we are of a work or calling, the more sure we can be that we have to do it."
— Steven Pressfield

What is it that's really staring you in the face from just behind the blank page? Pressfield names it "Resistance," and in so doing he steals back Resistance's power over us. He defines Resistance in such a thorough way that we're sure to recognize it the next time it makes an unwelcome appearance. And such appearances are inevitable, so it would serve us well to learn how to fight Resistance now because it's a war we'll be fighting for the rest of our writing lives.

The chapters are sometimes shockingly short, but pack the power of a Bruce Lee one-inch punch. In other words, you can certainly read the book in one sitting, but I wouldn't recommend it. Consider taking a few sections at a time, then truly leaning into Pressfield's challenging words to see where Resistance might be curtailing your writing. *The War of Art* is the most demanding, yet most encouraging, book I've read as a creative and a writer.

2. *Journal of a Novel: The East of Eden Letters*

blke.co/1ybX58J

"A book is like a man—clever and dull, brave and cowardly, beautiful and ugly. For every flowering thought there will be a page like a wet and mangy mongrel, and for every looping flight a tap on the wing and a reminder that wax cannot hold the feathers firm too near the sun."
— John Steinbeck

Journal of a Novel, which wasn't supposed to be published, collects Steinbeck's diary-like entries to his editor during the writing of *East of Eden*, what many critics consider to be his masterpiece (and one of my all-time favorite books).

Journal presents an unvarnished glimpse into Steinbeck's process as well as his fascinating internal wrestling with how the book might be received. For a writer who had received an astounding amount of acclaim for his career up to the point at which he wrote *East of Eden*, it's encouraging to every writer to see that even literary behemoth John Steinbeck had to fight Resistance.

3. *Bird by Bird: Some Instructions on Writing and Life*

http://blke.co/1Fnqqzy

"You own everything that happened to you. Tell your stories. If people wanted you to write warmly about them, they should have behaved better."
— Anne Lamott

For the writer, life and writing go hand in hand. A writer cannot separate herself from the writing any more than she could from her life. To live is to write; to write is to live. Sure, it's heavy-handed, but writer after writer espouses the same belief that they'd keep writing, even if there was no one left to read their books. That's why it's common to come across books like Anne Lamott's, where thoughts on writing coalesce with thoughts on living, although Lamott's book is the most uncommon of these types you'll read.

With her characteristic wit and humor, Lamott offers an encouraging, candid, hope-laden glimpse into both the craft of writing as well as the art of living a life from which to write.

4. *Walking on Water: Reflections on Faith and Art*

blke.co/1xSjlVf

"We don't want to feel less when we have finished a book; we want to feel that new possibilities of being have been opened to us. We don't want to close a book with a sense that life is totally unfair and that there is no light in the darkness; we want to feel that we have been given illumination."
— Madeline L'Engle

Though specifically talking to Christians in pursuit of creativity, L'Engle's ruminations serve as inspiration for all creatives. She speaks to what it means to create on a soul level, and how a writer can learn to listen and be aware in order to respond to the world around them through the creation of art. Though not targeted at writers, L'Engle found her creative release through the written word, so much of what she shares is from her personal experience.

Walking on Water may help writers of all kinds arrive at helpful, life-giving answers to the eternally existential questions of the writer: "Am I a writer?" and "Why am I writing?"

5. *Steal Like an Artist: 10 Things Nobody Told You About Being Creative*

blke.co/1xzFpQQ

"Draw the art you want to see, start the business you want to run, play the music you want to hear, write the books you want to read, build the products you want to use— do the work you want to see done."

— Austin Kleon

Austin Kleon's book can be easily read in one sitting, but like *The War of Art*, I suggest taking it in small doses. Delightfully presented with Kleon's graphic design background in full use, *Steal Like an Artist* offers ten tips for better, *productive* creativity. Ranging from "Write the Book You Want to Read" to "The Secret: Do Good Work and Share It with People," *Steal* makes the case that none of our ideas are original, but that certainly shouldn't prevent us from pursuing the work we're called to do.

If done well and done smartly, we'll eventually find our voice and ourselves within the art we "steal."

To Be Self-Published

If you want to learn the technical aspects of self-publishing and strategies for marketing yourself, these straightforward books offer superb teaching.

1. *Write. Publish. Repeat.*

blke.co/1trz5s0

"Success comes from hard work

and the accumulation of small numbers."

—Sean Platt

How-to books on self-publishing abound on Amazon, so it can be challenging to know where to begin. *Write. Publish. Repeat.* is likely the most thorough and lengthiest of them, but it's a useful, easy-to-read resource that can help any first-time, self-publishing author.

Written by Johnny B. Truant, Sean Platt, and David Wright, who weekly produce the (often explicit) Self-Publishing Podcast (selfpublishingpodcast.com), the book offers proven strategies for self-publishing.

2. *How to Format Your Novel for Kindle, Nook, the iBookstore, Smashwords, and CreateSpace . . . In One Afternoon (for Mac)*

blke.co/1trz87h

"Your book's appearance should reflect the care and effort you put into writing it."

— Ed Ditto

Formatting is an immensely important part of the self-publishing process. Ed Ditto's book was a much-needed help to me during the creation of my first self-published book, and I still refer back to his helpful tips and screen captures when formatting books today. If you use Scrivener to compile your books, Ditto's book offers step-by-step help. Plus, when I ran into a specific problem, I contacted him through EdDitto.com and he responded within a day—something I didn't expect, but was glad to have received.

If you're not a Scrivener user, I greatly recommend searching for a formatting book that will help you create the most professional-looking book possible. Readers will notice when a book just doesn't look right.

3. *Let's Get Digital / Let's Get Visible*

blke.co/1xXsQUD / blke.co/1trzgnk

"The Internet has revolutionized every business it has come into contact with, and publishing is no different. For the first time, these changes are handing power back to the writer. It's up to YOU if you want to profit from them."
— David Gaughran

David Gaughran's *Let's Get Digital* covers the basics of self-publishing and provides practical advice on editing, cover design, formatting, pricing, marketing, platform-building, and best practices for selling fiction and nonfiction. Its second, updated edition was released in September 2014.

Let's Get Visible offers invaluable information about Amazon's algorithms and rankings. While it doesn't give you the carefully hidden key to unlock Amazon's system, *Visible* does provide practical tips on how to make the most of your book being available through the world's largest book distributor.

4. ***How to Market a Book***

blke.co/1vJpIvl

"Marketing isn't a skill that most authors have naturally, and there is little formal training. But when your book hits the shelves, and the sales don't start rolling in, there's only two things an author can do. Keep writing more books and ... Get to grips with marketing."

— Joanna Penn

Joanna Penn's marketing book is well reviewed, and she has the sales numbers to prove her methods. Penn offers necessary help to writers who'd rather shun marketing. Although most writers simply want to write, self-publishing necessitates that authors also learn how to sell, and twenty-first-century selling can take hundreds of forms. She covers basic marketing principles, what an author should do to prepare him- or herself for success, short-term and long-term marketing plans, and book launches.

5. *Business for Authors*

blke.co/15nMcqc

"I'm not here to talk about creativity or the craft of writing in this book. My aim is to take the result of your creativity into the realm of actually paying the bills."
— Joanna Penn

Eschewing the technical details of what it takes to self-publish and diving into the many ways that self-publishers can earn a living, *Business for Authors* is a straightforward book that preaches what Penn successfully practices.

She reveals what's worked for her in becoming a full-time author-entrepreneur by delving into topics like turning your manuscript into multiple products (and thus multiple streams of income), working with other professionals to help you keep creating and producing, book marketing, and learning how to manage your money. If you're serious about turning your writing into a career, this is a great book to begin reading.

NOW READ, THEN WRITE!

"Of making many books there is no end,
and much study wearies the body."
— Ecclesiastes 12:12

By no means are these lists comprehensive. There are many fine books about writing that I have yet to read, like the oft-cited *Writing Down the Bones* (blke.co/1vKM3Zt). However, I've read nearly every one of the books listed and have found them invaluable to my maturation as a writer. I can only hope that when I finally venture into composing fiction that the storytelling books I've read will likewise prove beneficial.

If you'd like to peruse my virtual shelf of writing books, visit my GoodReads "On Writing" shelf at blke.co/gronwriting, sorted by rating, which features helpful books about writing, self-publishing, and freelancing.

If you've read a book on writing that's not on this list but you think should be, recommend it to me at blake@editfor.me. Otherwise, I hope these books might fill in the gaps where your writing work may have holes.

But always remember—don't let reading about writing prevent you from writing. While these books are helpful, there's no teacher like consistent practice.

THANK YOU

Thank *you* for reading and for supporting independent authors and publishing professionals.

Thank you to my patient wife. I'm so glad that God's edits on my life resulted in finding you. (And maybe the next book will be the one you really want me to write.)

Thank you to my editor, Alison Frenzel, for her efficient work and superb suggestions (alisonfrenzelcreative.com). Whatever errors remain in this book are certainly all mine.

Thank you to my editing and writing clients. I'm honored to have helped your words see the world.

Thank you to Jim Woods (jimwoodswrites.com) for the initial idea for the book, and to **Chris Morris** (chrismorriswrites.com) and **Kent Sanders** (kentsanders.net) for writerly encouragement.

Thank you to the Writers Unite (facebook.com/groups/WritersUniteGroup) **and Tribe Writers Facebook groups**. Your collective feedback helped immensely.

Thank you to Awaken Creativity, Art House Dallas's (arthousedallas.com) first writers group. There are few events I'm happier to see on my schedule than meeting and discussing writing with all of you.

ABOUT THE AUTHOR

Blake Atwood is a ridiculously fortunate husband and father who makes his living as a ghostwriter, editor, and author.

In addition to *Don't Fear the Reaper*, Blake wrote *The Gospel According to Breaking Bad*, has co-written or ghostwritten a handful of nonfiction books, and has edited dozens of manuscripts for self-publishing authors.

He delights in helping first-time and indie authors see their hard-won words find their way into the world. He also enjoys assisting busy professionals craft compelling content through ghostwritten books, articles, and blogs.

To learn more about how he may be able to help you on your writing project, contact him at BlakeAtwood.com/contact, or email him at blake@editfor.me.

READY FOR MORE?

Join ALL APPRENTICES,

a weekly email newsletter

curated by Blake Atwood

featuring the week's best writing about writing.

Subscribe at AllApprentices.com.

Made in the USA
Middletown, DE
18 September 2016